CONSTRUCTING AND RESISTING MODERNITY: MADRID 1900-1936

SUSAN LARSON

La Casa de la Riqueza
Estudios de la Cultura de España

20

CONSTRUCTING AND RESISTING MODERNITY: MADRID 1900-1936

SUSAN LARSON

La Casa de la Riqueza
Estudios de la Cultura de España, 20

IBEROAMERICANA · VERVUERT · 2011

Library of Congress Cataloging-in-Publication Data

Larson, Susan, 1968-
  Constructing and resisting modernity : Madrid, 1900-1936 / Susan Larson.
      p. cm. -- (La casa de la riqueza. Estudios de la cultura de España ; 20
  Includes bibliographical references and index.
  ISBN 978-1-936353-04-0 (acid-free paper) -- ISBN 978-8484895572 (acid-free paper)
  1. Madrid (Spain)--History--20th century. 2. Madrid (Spain)--Intellectual life--
20th century. 3. Popular culture--Spain--Madrid--History--20th century. 4. City planning--
Spain--Madrid--History--20th century. 5. Urbanization--Spain--Madrid--History--
20th century. I. Title.
  DP361.L37 2011
  946'.41074--dc22

                                                                  2011011962

© Iberoamericana, 2011
Amor de Dios, 1 – E-28014 Madrid
Tel.: +34 91 429 35 22 – Fax: +34 91 429 53 97

© Iberoamericana Vervuert Publishing Corp., 2011
9040 Bay Hill Blvd. – Orlando, FL 32819 USA
Tel:. +1 407 217 5534 – Fax.: +1 407 217 5059

Vervuert, 2011
Elisabethenstr. 3-9 – D-60594 Frankfurt am Main
Tel.: +49 69 597 46 17 – Fax: +49 69 597 87 43

info@iberoamericanalibros.com – www.ibero-americana.net

ISBN 978-84-8489-557-2 (Iberoamericana Editorial Vervuert)
ISBN 978-1-936353-04-0 (Iberoamericana Vervuert Publishing Corp.)

Depósito Legal: SE-3239-2011

Frontispice: Alfonso, "Colocación de una jácena. Edificio de Gran Vía".
© 2011 Artists Rights Society (ARS), New York / VEGAP, Madrid
Cover design: Carlos Zamora
Layout design: Carlos del Castillo

Table of Contents

Acknowledgements

This book is the product of a long and rich process of reading, writing and conversation. I take this opportunity to thank the always generous Malcolm Compitello, with whom I first talked through many of the concepts contained here. David Herzberger, William Sherzer, Judith Nantell and Joan Gilabert kindly read and commented on this project in a much earlier form. What Eva Woods Peiró has taught me about the possibilities of theorizing early film has been a revelation. Likewise, Matt Feinberg's clear articulation of Lefebvre's notion of social space provided me with another important "aha!" moment. My colleagues in the University of Kentucky Department of Geography and the Committee on Social Theory have also been a source of inspiration every time I cross disciplinary lines to raid their turf. Most of all, my undergraduate and graduate students at Fordham University and the University of Kentucky have provided me with the kind of intellectual connection and exchange that give true purpose to what I do.

This book would not have been possible without the help and expertise of Marga Lobo and Javier Herrera of the Spanish National Film Archive. Likewise, Carlos Sambricio, in addition to being cited several times, was helpful in the procurement of several of the images and maps included in this study. Jeff Levy and Dick Gilbreath at the University of Kentucky Gyula Pauer Center for Cartography were dedicated collaborators in the creation of the diagrams and maps that accompany Chapters Three, Four and Five. Mark Lauersdorf provided much-needed technical advice in the Tech Atelier. Funding from the Office of the Dean of Arts and Sciences at the University of Kentucky was also essential to the publication of this book. I want to thank my friend and colleague Ana Rueda for her unfailing support while this manuscript was being prepared. Finally, I am indebted to the careful attention to detail of Klaus Vervuert and Kerstin Houba, who found this book a home.

CHAPTER I

Modern Madrid as Force and Form

One of geography's main concerns is the study of places, but questions dealing with a sense of place are also central to the inquiries of other disciplines. Place is ultimately a matter of ideology, an inherently subjective concept, and it does not yield well to instruments of science, or even of social science. When one takes a step back and looks at representations of place and urban space in particular, one often finds that they play a reciprocal role in the creation of the urban environment itself. City planners and architects need some image, some concept to inspire them as they set about creating new urban environments in which people work and live. The experience of living in the urban environment, in turn, becomes the content for much of modern culture, which portrays the city in a myriad of ways, some critical, some utopian, but always with a sense of the power it has in shaping people's lives.

Metropolis and Madrid

Metropolis (1927) is a case in point. One of the most widely distributed films of the late 1920s, it was released in Madrid in 1928 and presented a variety of images of the modern metropolis that from all accounts movie-going *madrileños* superimposed onto their own city. Relatively late to arrive in Madrid, when the film was first shown there was already a built-up excitement through the word of mouth generated by those who had seen it abroad. One example of the creation of this anticipation can be found in Luis Buñuel's review of the film in *La Gaceta Literaria* (May 1, 1927). While harshly critical of the screenplay penned by Lang's wife Thea von Harbou, Buñuel praises what he calls "el fondo plástico-fotogénico del film... 'Metrópolis' colmará todas las medidas, nos asombrará como el más maravilloso libro de imágenes que se ha compuesto" (6) [the plastic and photogenic depth of the film... 'Metropolis' will exceed all expectations, will thrill us as much as the most marvelous book of images that has ever been written.][1] The real genius behind the film, according to Buñuel, is the architect Otto Hunte, who "nos anonda con su colosal visión de la ciudad del año 2000. Podrá ser equivocada, incluso anticuada con relación a últimas teorizaciones sobre la ciudad del porvenir, pero, desde el punto de vista fotogénico, es innegable su inédita y sorprendente belleza; de tan perfecta técnica, que puede sufrir un prolongado examen sin que por un solo instante se descubra la maqueta" (6) [overwhelms us with his colossal vision of the city of the year 2000. It may be incorrect, or even outdated in light of recent theories of the city of the future, but, from a visual standpoint, such surprising beauty has never been seen before; it is so technically perfect that one can look very carefully without even noticing the scale model in the background].

While some *madrileños* had most likely already read reviews of the film and accounts such as this, others saw the film announced via this advertisement *(Fig. 1.1)* for the screenings in the Real Cinema and the Príncipe Alfonso Theater or *cinematógrafos*, as they were then called. "Metropolis: La ciudad sobre las ciudades" reads the poster.[2] It grants

---

1. All translations are those of the author unless otherwise noted.
2. This image promoted Lang's film through January of 1928 in *El Sol*, a liberal Madrid newspaper founded in 1917 by Nicolás María de Urgoiti with the collaboration of José Ortega y Gasset.

the architect Otto Hunte as much credit for the film as the director, and well it should, for the look of the film and the figure of the imagined city of the title had a striking impact on viewers.[3] The city of the film is divided into three parts, one being "high above, a pleasure garden for the sons of the masters of the metropolis," according to the intertitles. It houses the gardens where the children of capitalists seem not to have a care in the world. This is also the most technologically advanced stratum with its skyscrapers, bird-like airplanes and graceful, smooth vehicles carrying the lucky few back and forth in speed and comfort. Freedom of expression and freedom from work go hand in hand. Within this lofty paradise the business of capital accumulation takes place. The film draws us into the building of John Frederson, "Master of Metropolis," the hardworking taskmaster whose office is located inside a massive clock, granting him the role of a modern god of progress and efficiency.

The business of production and distribution takes place in the second part of the city, underground, where the workers toil in the factories. Every last one of them suffers from fatigue. They are so exhausted that simple communication is impossible. They have no names and dress identically. The workers see none of the fruits of their labor, spending their time engaged in a hopeless battle with unrelenting machines. One of the most memorable scenes of the movie is an expressionistic one where a factory machine is suddenly, in young Freder's dream, transformed into the vengeful god Moloch who demands living sacrifices of the workers, who march in unison into his mouth and are swallowed alive. The third and lowest level is where the workers are housed, as the intertitle tells us, "far below the surface of the earth."

Freder, after having fallen in love at first sight with María, a woman from the worker's realm, comes into contact for the first time with the harsh reality of the workers, whose collective plight is largely the responsibility of his father. He and the revolutionary María

---

3. For details on how Lang's film *Metropolis* was received in Spain and elsewhere see Jensen and Jenkins.

come to share a sense of justice when they find themselves in a position to bring about the beginning of an understanding between the workers and capitalist management. The film's ultimately conservative position is based on Plato's argument for the separation of mankind into the philosopher/ruling, guardian/middle and working (slave) classes in the *Republic*.[4] "Between the brain that plans and the hands that build there must be a mediator. It is the heart that must bring about an understanding between them," says María during a quasi-religious meeting of the workers. The film concludes with young Freder, the enlightened capitalist innocent of any crime against his working-class brothers, playing a Messianic role. He takes the hand of his father and that of the worker's chief foreman and joins them together. In the last frame of the film he tells us "there can be understanding between the hands and the brain when the heart acts as mediator." What in purely visual terms had all the makings of a powerful indictment of the dehumanization of the masses by an increasingly industrialized and profit-driven society ultimately becomes a film affirming bourgeois ideology.

It is worth noting that the double meaning of the advertising slogan "La ciudad sobre las ciudades," which can mean "The City Above All Other Cities" or at the same time "The City About [i.e., representing] All Other Cities" on this Spanish poster mentions only the highest layer of the city, the wealthy metropolis of ease and power. After Spanish moviegoers saw the film, when they left the movie theaters and stepped out into the street, they were located in the very center of Madrid's newly-constructed version of the metropolis of money, power and entertainment where any evidence of the process of how the space was created was hidden from sight, down below, literally in the working-class neighborhoods of Cuatro Caminos and Carabanchel, and, figuratively, in the economic order of things. Madrid's urban planning between 1890 and 1936 was focused almost

---

4. For modern interpretations of this division of the city/body and its political and philosophical implications see Reed and Williams.

exclusively on the construction of spaces where institutions of power
and a new leisure industry would be housed – iconic spaces whose
existence was intended to prove that Madrid was just as modern as
other major urban centers.

Culture, whether intentionally or not, often affirms the ideological
framework from which it arises. Film in particular, with its relatively
large budgets, is a medium almost entirely dependent on the marketplace. Modern city planning functions on an even grander scale. In
these pages we will look at how Madrid's city planners in the late nineteenth and early twentieth centuries often thought of themselves as
Freder-like intermediaries playing a progressive role in the creation of
urban space. Assuming that the creation of real space is inseparable
from its representation, this study looks at narratives written by authors
whose dystopian representations of the city suggested alternative ways
to navigate urban space. Both urban planners and authors of fiction
responded to the effects of modernization in Madrid and shared common concerns. They considered many of the same problems, albeit in
dramatically different ways. Madrid in the nineteenth and twentieth
centuries was simultaneously planned for renovation and destruction
and it is because of this inherently modern situation that the Spanish
capital, like all urban centers, was the site of intense political and social
struggle. To understand how this struggle played out in both material
and symbolic terms is to understand the history of the Spanish capital and its experience of modernity.

What is Spanish Modernity?

Philosophers have often used architectural and planning metaphors
to discuss the challenges of modernity. In the first issue of the *Revista
de Occidente*, dated July of 1923, José Ortega y Gasset clearly positions the magazine as an essential emissary of the modern in Spain.[5]

---

5. López-Campillo goes into detail in *'La Revista de Occidente' y la formación de
   minorías 1923-1936* about the role that Ortega's publication had in the forma-

In this first issue Ortega unveils the mission of the magazine, which would soon become one of Spain's most influential sources of philosophical, political and social theory. The *Revista de Occidente* was necessary, in his words, because

> [E]n la sazón presente adquiere mayor urgencia este afán de conocer 'por dónde va el mundo', pues surgen dondequiera los síntomas de una profunda transformación en las ideas, en los sentimientos, en las maneras, en las instituciones. Muchas gentes comienzan a sentir la penosa impresión de ver su existencia invadida por el caos. Y, sin embargo, un poco de claridad, otro poco de orden y suficiente jerarquía en la información les revelaría pronto el plano de la nueva arquitectura en que la vida occidental se está reconstruyendo. (2)

> [At this present moment the desire to know 'where the world is going' acquires more urgency than ever, since there is a profound sense that everywhere there is a transformation in ideas, in sentiment, in behavior, in institutions. Many people are beginning to get the troubled sense that their existence is being invaded by chaos. In spite of this, a little bit of clarity, a little bit of order and enough hierarchy of information would soon reveal to them the design of the new architectural model which Western life is reconstructing.]

Clarity, order, hierarchy, structure: this was what Ortega sought to provide in an increasingly chaotic world. Ortega, much like the urban planners and architects we will look at in the coming pages, saw the entirety of Western life as an ongoing architectural project reshaping a complex map that was unreadable without the guidance and knowledge of a master philosopher. What Ortega articulates here is a desire to enter into the polemic of modernity as experienced not just in Spain but in the rest of the Western world. This first issue contains essays by Spaniards such as Pío Baroja who writes on travel, Ortega on the Romanian-French poet Anna de Noailles, and Fernando

----

tion of an intellectual elite that would fragment into subgroups at the outbreak of the Spanish Civil War.

Vela, who writes a scientific article entitled "El individuo y el medio: nuevas ideas biológicas" [The Individual and His Environment: New Biological Ideas].

What is most telling about this first issue of the *Revista de Occidente* is the inclusion of what was to become a regular section called "Nuevos hechos, nuevas ideas" [New Accomplishments, New Ideas], meant to be a showcase of recent theories and ideas from other countries. Prominently featured was an essay by one of the forefathers of the discipline of sociology, Georg Simmel. His work focused on how to psychologically and intellectually respond to the vast array of experiences and stimuli of modern life. He often wrote about the effects of rapid urbanization on humankind's sense of space and time and its need to submit to new, strict orderings of these governing principles.[6] His essay in this first *Revista*, translated into Spanish as "Filosofía de la moda" [The Philosophy of Fashion], focuses specifically on the issues of social dependence, individual liberty and class within the context of a discussion of fashion. He develops his concept of "la vida como dualismo" [the dual nature of life], through which he finds that in modern life, it is "precisamente en su dualismo que descubrimos la unidad de la vida íntegra" [precisely in its dualism that we discover the unity of a complete life] (1923: 47). His theorizing on the most abstract of issues based on the everyday details of life comes from his then-groundbreaking sociological approach that inspired many of the theorists who subsequently went on to develop the models for conducting cultural analysis that will be undertaken in the present study.

Fashion is completely arbitrary for Simmel: "con que una vez ordena lo que es útil, otra lo incomprensible, otra la estética o prácticamente inocuo, revela su perfecta indiferencia hacia las normas prácticas, racionales, de la vida" [because sometimes it orders the useful, sometimes the incomprehensible, and other times the aesthetic or practically innocuous, it reveals its perfect indifference to the practical and

---

6. For a synthesis of these concepts see Simmel's 1903 essay 'Die Großstadt und das Geistesleben' [The Metropolis and Mental Life.]

rational norms of life] (1923: 48). Central to his theory is the assertion
that fashion plays an important role in capitalist society, the idea of
what is fashionable trickling down from the wealthier to the working
classes, in reality unattainable but at the same time highly desirable
because "la intervención del capitalismo no puede menos que acelerar
vivamente este proceso y mostrarlo al desnudo, porque los objetos de
moda, fuera de cosas externas, son muy particularmente asequibles
por el simple dinero" [the intervention of capitalism can do no less
than actively accelerate this process and lay it bare, because fashionable objects, aside from being superficial objects, are popularly accessible through everyday money] (1923: 51).[7] In this way Simmel uses
fashion, as symptomatic of modernity, to show how the modern is
linked to purely symbolic capital and how this affects every modern
citizen on an individual level.[8]

> Es específico de la vida moderna un 'tempo' impaciente, el cual indi-
> ca no sólo el ansia de rápida mutación en los contenidos cualitativos de la
> vida, sino el vigor cobrado por el atractivo formal de cuanto es límite, del
> comienzo y del fin, del llegar y no irse. El caso más compendioso de este
> linaje es la moda, que, por su juego ante la tendencia a una expansión
> total y el aniquilamiento de su propio sentido que esta expansión acarrea,
> adquiere el atractivo peculiar de los límites y extremos, el atractivo de un
> comienzo y un fin simultáneos de la novedad y al mismo tiempo de la

---

7.   A discussion of fashion appears in Chapter Four of this study in conjunction with
     an analysis of Díaz Fernández's *La Venus mecánica* in light of the criticism of
     York and Gronow. Unlike these late twentieth-century scholars, however, Simmel
     does not believe that any true resistance to the dominant ideals of an elitist
     modern culture is possible.
8.   The use of the term 'symbolic capital' here comes from Bourdieu's discussion of
     it on pages 171-183 of his *Outline of a Theory of Practice*. According to the soci-
     ological anthropologist Bourdieu, symbolic capital can be found, in his words,
     'in the work of reproducing established relations – through feasts, ceremonies,
     exchanges of gifts, visits or courtesies and above all, marriages – which is no less
     vital to the existence of the group than the reproduction of the economic bases
     of its existence, the labor required to conceal the function of the exchanges is as
     important an element as the labor needed to carry out the function' (171).

caducidad. Su cuestión no es 'ser o no ser', sino que es ella a un tiempo
ser y no ser, está siempre en la divisoria de las aguas que van al pasado y al
futuro, y, merced a ello, nos proporciona durante su vigencia una sensación de actualidad más fuerte que casi todas las demás cosas. (58)

[The impatient 'tempo' which is a characteristic of modern life
demonstrates not only an anxiety about the rapid change in the qualita-
tive content of life, but the energy given over to the overall sense of arriv-
ing and never having left. The most encompassing example of this is
fashion, which, because of the game it plays as its influence expands and
the way that it outdates itself, acquires the unique trait of knowing the
limits and extremes, the attractiveness of a simultaneous beginning and
end, of being simultaneously new and outdated. Its central question is not
'to be or not to be,' but to be and at the same time not to be, so it is always
on the dividing line between the past and the future, and because of this,
as long as it lasts fashion provides us a sense of the present that is much
stronger than other things.]

Even "anti-moda" [anti-fashion], as Simmel later calls it, the conscious need to be different from the crowd, is seen as dependent upon
the commonly-accepted concept of fashion. To understand and
accept the inevitability of this dualism was to accept the modern condition. This modern obsession with the superficial and the tendency
of the moneyed classes to pass this sense of the here and now on to
others was a great fear of intellectuals who were living in a time when
culture was becoming increasingly commodified and the avant-garde
was reinventing itself at a quickening rate in Spain just as in the rest
of Europe.[9] Couched in terms of a concern for the loss of a sense of

---

9. For Poggioli in his *The Theory of the Avant-Garde,* an ever-changing avant-garde
   is part of the mechanical twentieth century, a 'law of nature for contemporary
   and modern art' (1968: 225). In the conclusion to his work he shows how
   every artistic generation thinks it has the last word and that those who think
   the avant-garde as an aesthetic is being overcome are mistaken. 'It is obvious
   that the very dialectic of movements and the effect of fashion cause every avant-
   garde to be able (or pretend to be able) to transcend not only the academy and
   tradition but also the avant-garde preceding it. Sometimes a movement fools

history, both Ortega and Simmel consistently warned against the potential dangers of democratization in the form of the mixing of high and low culture.

As can be seen throughout the first issue of the *Revista de Occidente*, Ortega was entrenched in the Enlightenment belief that there was one possible answer to any question, that the world could be ordered, represented and explained correctly for the betterment of society as a whole. He thought of himself as a conduit of modernity — as someone who through his influential words and editorial activities could carry this ideology to and from Spain. There were radically different, more progressive and democratic ideologies of the modern in circulation in early twentieth-century Spain, however, as we will see when we take a look at the critical theory and novels of José Díaz Fernández. Unlike Díaz Fernández, Ortega would maintain his highly influential top-down view of modernity long after the irrationality and the horror of the damage his countrymen inflicted upon one another during the Spanish Civil War of 1936-39.

Central to many debates on the nature of modernity (and by extension postmodernity) is the question of whether or not we have broken with the ideals of the Enlightenment.[10] Throughout the twentieth century philosophers have been asking difficult questions about the nature of concepts such as progress, reason, and the potential of science to improve the human condition. Architectural historians put

---

itself into believing it attains the peak and end point of all avant-gardism in its own action, believing that it realizes and represents, all by itself, the ultimate intention and the ultimate stage of avant-gardism' (1968: 220). The use of the word avant-garde here is in accordance with this constantly self-generating type of artistic movement which forms an inherent part of the modern period and not the concept of the avant-garde as a historical period that is put forth, for example, in Bürger's *Theory of the Avant-Garde*.

10. The work of Habermas, formed in conjunction with and as a reaction to the work of the Frankfurt School philosophers, wants to salvage the Enlightenment project out of fear of its complete abandonment which he thinks would bring about a world given over to totalitarianism and nihilism. For a thorough assessment of Habermas's attitude towards the Enlightenment and its legacy see Bernstein.

their concern in spatial terms: if the architects of Auschwitz had been inspired by the building principles of the Bauhaus in their efficient design, if society was progressing along a rational path towards a society that was the best for the greatest number, what went so horribly wrong? The Enlightenment seemed to have turned upon itself and transformed the human quest for emancipation into a system of universal oppression in the name of liberation. This is the thesis of Max Horkheimer and Theodor Adorno's 1947 *Dialectic of the Enlightenment* wherein the two philosophers argue that the logic that lies behind Enlightenment rationality hides a logic of domination and oppression. Inherent in the desire to dominate nature (in the guise of technological progress), they wrote, was the drive to dominate human beings. They saw as the only way out a revolt of nature, which had to be perceived as a revolt of human nature against the oppressive power of purely instrumental reason over culture and individual personality.

Subsequent thinkers interested in space and society who want to salvage what was potentially civilizing about the Enlightenment (ideas of emancipation, our ability to change ourselves and our environment, participation in democracy) by extension tend to be pessimistic about the possibility of realizing such a project under contemporary economic and political conditions. Any real change to society, any effort to make it more humane, many argue, has to be tied to the struggle against an overarching material and symbolic structure that orders our existence today: capitalism. One particularly moving attempt to capture the modern experience that simultaneously locates that experience solidly within capitalism can be found in Marshall Berman's *All That is Solid Melts Into Air. The Experience of Modernity*:

> There is a mode of vital experience—experience of space and time, of the self and others, of life's possibilities and perils—that is shared all over the world today. I will call this body of experience 'modernity.' To be modern is to find ourselves in an environment that promises us adventure, power, joy, growth, transformation of ourselves and of the world—and, at the very same time, that threatens to destroy everything we have, everything we know, everything we are. Modern environments

and experiences cut across all boundaries of geography and ethnicity, of class and nationality, of religion and ideology: in this sense, modernity can be said to unite all mankind. But it is a paradoxical unity, a unity of disunity: it pours us all into a maelstrom of perpetual disintegration and renewal, of struggle and contradiction, of ambiguity and anguish. To be modern is to be part of a universe in which, as Marx said, 'all that is sold melts into air.' (1982: 15)

This struggle and upheaval due to the constant changes brought about by the comings and goings of capital always bring one back to the city, the producer and the product of the capitalist system in which we are so entrenched it sometimes becomes invisible. A cultural and geographical study of Madrid can make visible the creative and destructive forces of urban capital and how different kinds of artistic representations of this situation can both support and contradict widely-accepted ideas about the city's modern experience.

Hispanists writing about modernity always need to confront the question: is Spain's modernity significantly different from the modernities of countries in other parts of the world? On one level the answer can only be yes, since the experience of each country, each region and each individual stems from a set of unique circumstances. One look at recent titles of publications on Hispanic modernity and the Enlightenment, however, shows us that these intertwined concepts are almost always linked to a series of problematizing adjectives such as "insufficient" (Subirats), "recalcitrant" (Delgado, Mendelson, Vásquez), "marginal" (Geist and Monleón), "multiple" (Eisenstadt), "divergent" (Ramos), "quixotic" (Ciallella), and "peripheral" (Larson), with the word "modernities" oftentimes appearing in the plural form. There are many differing ideas about the nature of Spain's entrance into the modern world. In *La ilustración insuficiente* Eduardo Subirats is of the opinion that, intellectually speaking, Spain is poorly equipped to understand and fully partake in the development of the modern, industrial West because

[l]a Ilustración española, considerada como movimiento filosófico, fue una época pobre, tímida en sus posiciones, poco decidida en sus críticas

y respuestas, diletante en su actividad investigadora que nunca supo definir con el suficiente vigor la misma idea de la modernidad por ella inaugurada. (1990: 24)

[the Spanish Enlightenment, when considered as a philosophical movement, was so impoverished, so timid in its positions, so undecided in its criticisms and answers, so unprofessional in its research activity that it was never able to define with sufficient energy the idea of modernity that it had inaugurated.]

Subirats cites Ortega several times, both men negating the importance of the Enlightenment in Spain, refusing to acknowledge its importance to twentieth-century Spanish thought. For Subirats, Spain is intellectually, socially and economically different from the rest of Europe, and special attention needs to be paid to these differences when talking about Spain's modern development. An entirely different position can be found in Juan Pablo Fusi and Jordi Palafox's more historical approach to Spanish modernity in *España 1808-1996: El desafío de la modernidad*. The authors stress how Spain in purely economic and social terms is very much like the rest of Europe (especially the other Mediterranean countries) in the way the country faces modernity. The authors forcefully rail against what they call

estereotipos (la imagen romántica de España), crisis históricas (el desastre del 98, la guerra civil de 1936-1939, el franquismo) e interpretaciones historiográficas (fracaso de la revolución burguesa, fracaso de la revolución industrial) que pondrían el énfasis en el dramatismo de determinadas manifestaciones de la vida colectiva española y producirían una visión extremadamente pesimista y crítica de la España contemporánea; España como problema; España, país dramático; España como fracaso. [...] En otras palabras, consideramos a España como un 'país normal'. (1997: 11)

[stereotypes (the romantic image of Spain), historical crises (the Disaster of '98, the Civil War of 1936-39, Franquism) and historiographic interpretations (the failure of the bourgeois revolution, the failure of the industrial revolution) that would emphasize the drama of certain events of Spanish collective life and would produce an extremely pessimistic and critical view of contemporary Spain; Spain as a problem; Spain, a dramatic country; Spain as a failure. [...] In other words, we consider Spain to be a 'normal country.']

This book takes the position that focusing on Spain's unique historical circumstances yet considering these circumstances within and in comparison to a broadly industrialized West is necessary because capital is an increasingly global movement that links countries to each other economically and culturally, as we shall see in future chapters. Since capital becomes increasingly urbanized and the discourse of the urban seeks to redefine itself by recourse to the symbolic, some of the national distinctions weaken.

In her essay "Memory and Modernity in Democratic Spain" Jo Labanyi sums up the situation when she acknowledges that the notion that there is a single monolithic model of modernity – that of the nations of Northern Europe – has been questioned by almost all cultural historians but that the underlying assumption by many historians still remains that some modernities are superior to others. "So long as modernity continues to be defined in terms of capitalist development, it presupposes a teleological scheme which, although it may evolve at different speeds, in some cases going via fascism or socialism, nevertheless has as its inevitable goal the establishment of global capitalism" (2007: 90-91). Labanyi goes on to encourage historians and cultural critics to reconsider modernity as a way of thinking about the present and the past and to separate modernity from modernization in order to make way for a serious consideration of memory.[11] Many of the critics mentioned above tackle the problem of

---

11. In 'Memory and Modernity in Democratic Spain' Labanyi argues that 'modernity is best understood not as the cultural expression of capitalist modernization, but as a particular set of relations of present to past' (2007: 89). While the goal of her essay is different from that of this study, the way that Labanyi categorizes the problems inherent in believing that Spain's modern 'belatedness' is linked to relative economic weakness in the nineteenth and twentieth centuries productively informs this argument.

Spain's modernity falling relatively low on the perceived hierarchy of Western European and Anglo-American modernities from the vantage point of postcolonial theories of periphery and center, emphasizing Spain's difference and otherness. This book is an experiment in what Madrid's modern experience looks like when seen through the lens of a materialist cultural geography.

What one finds, quite simply, is that Madrid and its myriad representations are remarkably similar to those of other major urban centers of the time. The first three decades of the twentieth century in Spain saw a period of exceptional urban development when Madrid began in earnest to become an internationally-known modern metropolis and capital. As a city it sought an identity for itself and during this defining period Madrid's literature is contradictory in its attitudes towards the city. An analysis of culture produced in and about the city of Madrid during this period that ties it closely to the urban environment for and in which it was produced makes us take notice of certain authors heretofore neglected (here Carmen de Burgos, José Díaz Fernández and Andrés Carranque de Ríos) whose images of the city force us to reexamine both the rules of cultural production of the period and the geography of Madrid which makes them possible.

The Urban Process

Anyone bridging the gap between the Humanities and the Social Sciences has to find his or her own way of bringing together the material and the symbolic or, what this chapter, inspired by the work of Franco Moretti, calls "force and form." The theories of modernity and modernization of Ortega and Simmel were written and read in a time more or less concurrent with our object of study: Madrid and various narratives of Madrid between 1900 and 1936. Henri Lefebvre's 1974 *Production de l'espace*, which links the themes of urbanization and modernity, was written in the aftermath of a similarly disruptive time. Some of Lefebvre's early writings on revolutionizing urban space were boiled down, shouted and used as slogans by those participating in the French student uprisings of May 1968. Lefebvre uses

the categories of the *perceived*, the *conceived* and the *lived* coupled
with the idea of the urban as a modern process, not as an object of
study fixed in time, but in order to illustrate his theory of social space.
To explain: he theorized the *perceived* as the spatial practices involved
in capitalist production and reproduction (one's understanding of the
nature of the urban built environment and one's place in it); the term
conceived he used to denote the representation of the city tied to relations of production (in other words, the spatial constructions of tech-
nocrats); while the *lived* described a dynamic of embracing or rejecting imaginative representations of the city (everyday, individual
reactions of artists to the freely-circulating images of the metropolis)
(1991: 147-168).

    Lefebvre's concept of culture has had an enormous influence on the
fields of Human and Cultural Geography. For the urban theorist, culture (meaning anything produced by the creative impulses of men and
women) is not a thing but rather a set of relations between things. As
such it is irrevocably bound to the concept of space which cannot be
considered a product among other products. In his essay "Social Space"
he shows how space, despite its production by creative impulses, cannot be reduced to a simple object because it subsumes the things produced, and encompasses their interrelationships in their coexistence,
in their relative order or disorder.[12] According to Lefebvre,

> there is nothing imagined, unreal or ideal about space as compared, for
> example, with science, representations, ideas or dreams. Itself the outcome
> of past actions, social space is what permits fresh actions to occur, while sug-
> gesting others and prohibiting yet others. Among these actions, some serve
> production, others consumption (i.e., the enjoyment of the fruits of pro-
> duction). Social space implies a great diversity of knowledge. (1991: 73)

The knowledge referred to here is that of the history of social relations behind the construction of space. It is this relational approach

---

12. The way Lefebvre used the term 'social space' when he wrote his essay in the early
    1970s can be likened to the way 'place' is used by cultural geographers in the
    1990s to the present day.

that allows us to begin to understand the spatial constructs of power at work in Madrid's urban planning and cultural responses to this creation and control of space. Consistently dialectical and bent on the study of modern life not as a fixed object but as a multi-faceted and ongoing process of human power relations, it is easy to understand how Lefebvre was known for being a thinker who provided his students with more questions than answers.

The historical-materialist theories of the urban geographer David Harvey are one attempt to answer and expand upon some of these very questions posed by Lefebvre. Harvey develops what he calls theories of the urbanization of capital and the urbanization of consciousness. Much of his work consists of outlining the material bases of objective space and time and showing how these concepts are inextricably bound to the urban and, in the twentieth century, the industrial. He makes his important contribution to Marxist thinking about modern life by adding the concept of urban space to materialist readings of modern culture. In the introduction to his 1985 *The Urban Experience*, he states: "Historical materialism has to be upgraded to historical-geographical materialism" (6). Harvey's theories go far towards answering questions such as: how does capital become urbanized? and, what are the consequences of this urbanization? Marx, Harvey and other materialist geographers assume that capitalism is inherently expansionary and technologically dynamic. Profit depends on the exploitation of living labor in production. This defines the central class relation and the struggle between buyers (capitalists) and sellers (workers) of labor power as a commodity. Increasingly, as time goes on, investments in new systems of transport and communication reduce spatial barriers and roll back the possible geographical boundaries of exchange relations. Though the movement of commodities is constrained by the cost and time of transportation, credit money begins to move as fast and with as few spatial constraints as information. Money, finance, and credit form hierarchically-organized central nervous systems regulating and controlling the circulation of capital and expressing a class interest largely through private action. Urban centers, therefore, are the centers of coordination, decision-making, and control, usually within a hierarchically-organized geographical structure. As Harvey summarizes:

> Capital flow presupposes tight temporal and spatial coordination in the midst of increasing separation and fragmentation. It is impossible to imagine such a material process without the production of some kind of urbanization as a 'rational landscape' within which the accumulation of capital can proceed. Capital accumulation and the production of urbanization go hand in hand. (1985: 22)

Central to Harvey's theories of the urbanization of capital and consciousness is the fact that in an industrial urban center production is typically separated from consumption by market exchanges. This has implications for urbanization and the urban structure because work spaces and times separate out from consumption spaces and times in ways unknown in an artisan or peasant culture. The moment of production, like that of consumption, becomes increasingly fragmented. Vacation, leisure and entertainment take place separate from the spaces of daily reproduction, a good filmic representation of this being found in the discussion of *Metropolis* earlier in this chapter. This spatial division of consumption required the construction of permanent social and physical spaces within and between urban centers and explains the dramatic reshaping of the city of Madrid during the late nineteenth and early twentieth centuries.

The Urbanization of Consciousness

Modernizing Spain was based on an increasingly urban society whose whole class structures were being redefined. Class warfare between capital and labor and the drive to reproduce that basic class relation of domination became the pivot of urban politics. Integrating migrants and absorbing shocks of technological change posed key questions of socioeconomic policy and political management. The role of women, for example, changed in both the labor market and in the household and the family had to readapt itself to the buying and selling of labor power as a way of life, as will be seen in many of the stories and short novels considered here. Historically, in the industrializing city the urban pot threatens to boil over, and urban planners and other municipal authorities were charged with finding some way of keeping the working class under control. The manipulation of space is a form of social power for all classes. Capitalism has to urbanize to reproduce itself but the urbanization of capital creates some dangerous contradictions. Both Lefebvre and Harvey assert that these serious problems can only be changed if they are treated as symptoms of the process of the urbanization of capital.

Since capitalism is a revolutionary mode of production, creatively and willfully destructive, always looking to develop new organizational forms, new technologies, new lifestyles, new modalities of production and exploitation, it depends on new social definitions of time and space. Significantly, Harvey does not see space and time as a duality. He thinks they are inextricably bound together and the glue that binds them, quite simply, is the mediation of money.[13] There is another part of Harvey's theory (and perhaps one of the most important for our purposes here) that needs to be explained before we embark on a discussion of the specifically Spanish situation, and that is his theory of place, the concept with which this chapter began. Building on Lefebvre's relational view of space-time, Harvey answers the question: by what social process(es) is place constructed? Harvey, reiterating his ideas on space-time, says that

> entities achieve relative stability in both their bounding and their internal ordering of processes creating space, for a time. Such permanences come to occupy a piece of space in an exclusive way (for a time) and thereby define a place – their place – (for a time). The process of place formation is a process of carving out 'permanences' from the flow of

---

13. In 'The Currency of Space-Time' (Chapter 10 of *Justice, Nature and the Geography of Difference*) Harvey explores the ideas of Whitehead and Leibniz on relational aspects of space and time as a counter to the absolute views of Newton and what Harvey calls the 'hegemonic' views of Kant. He chooses the former over the latter because he wants to emphasize and work with fluid, dialectical concepts of space and time rather than specific, static categories. Drawing on these two philosophers, he comes up with his own 'relational theory of space, place, and environment' (1996: 250-267).

processes creating spatio-temporality. But the 'permanences' – no matter
how solid they may seem – are not eternal but always subject to time as
'perpetual perishing.' They are contingent on processes of creation, sus-
tenance and dissolution. (1996: 261)

In other words, place is both a mere position or location within a
map of space-time constituted within some social process or an enti-
ty or "permanence" occurring within and transformative of the construction of space-time. In this way, one can understand the material-
ist-geographical concept of place as the site of the imaginary, as the
configuration of social relations, as the material manifestation of
power and as an element in discourse. The effect, according to Harvey, is "to understand places as internally heterogeneous, dialectical
and dynamic configurations of relative 'permanences' within the
overall spatio-temporal dynamics of socio-ecological processes"
(1996: 296).

A consciousness of place as defined by Harvey can be seen in written form in the chronotopes that Mikhail Bakhtin attributes to the
novel, for example. In *The Dialogic Imagination: Four Essays* (1981)
Bakhtin defines the chronotope as representative of the intrinsic con-
nectedness of temporal relationships that are artistically expressed in
literature. Bakhtin borrows the term from Einstein's Theory of Relativ-
ity almost as a metaphor: almost, but not entirely because, as Harvey
once again states, "time, as it were, thickens, takes on flesh, becomes
artistically visible" while "space becomes charged and responsive to the
movements of time, plot and history" (1996: 84). It is in this way that
places are constructed in human historical geography, through language, music, painting, and other forms of creative expression.

Hand in hand with modernity come new networks of places as
Harvey defines them, constituted as fixed capital embedded in the
land and configurations of organized social relations (institutions) and
new markets. Harvey points out that in this way "difference" and "otherness" are produced in space through the simple logic of uneven capital investment, a proliferating geographical division of labor, an
increasing segmentation of reproductive activities and the rise of spatially ordered (and often segregated) social distinctions (1996: 19-45).

Modernity's urban political and social struggles come about because the speculative element in these processes is very strong, often pitting one faction of capital against another. Smith points out the inherent unevenness of the process.

> The logic of uneven development derives specifically from the opposed tendencies, inherent in capital, towards the differentiation but simultaneous equalization of the levels and conditions of production. Capital is continually invested in the built environment in order to produce surplus value and expand the basis of capital itself. But equally, capital is continually withdrawn from the built environment so that it can move elsewhere and take advantage of higher profit rates. The spatial immobilization of productive capital in its material form is no more or less a necessity than the perpetual circulation of capital as value. (1996: xv)

What Smith posits here and what this study seeks to do are similar: both show how capital achieves the production of space in its own image. The unevenness of Madrid's modernization process is inherent in both the large-scale urban projects undertaken by those in power and the narrative responses of those authors critiquing the human costs of these reforms.

Harvey names this overwhelming change in time-space dimensionality "time-space compression," the experience of which, in his words, "forces all of us to adjust our notions of space and time and to rethink prospects for social action" (1996: 243). The avant-garde can be understood in this way, for example – as a group of artists who responded in a variety of revolutionary ways to these new experiences of space and time, so dramatic in rapidly-industrializing urban centers. Modern consciousness, then, is urbanized. As Harvey puts it,

> [t]o dissect the urban process in all of its fullness is to lay bare the roots of consciousness formation in the material realities of daily life. It is out of the complexities and perplexities of this experience that we build elementary understandings of the meanings of space and time; of social power and its legitimations; of forms of domination and social interaction; of the relation to nature through production and consumption; and of human nature, civil society, and political life. (1985: 230)

Drawing on the theoretical models of early sociologists (much of whose work dealt precisely with the urban and the modern like Simmel and Lefebvre) and the concept of mass culture as posited by the Frankfurt School, Harvey treats the urbanization of consciousness as a key political problem.

Charting the Relationship between Urban Conflict and Written Form

But how does one link the written word to urban space? All urban projects must exist in the imagination before they are realized in the world. Scholars inspired by materialist ideas have often been misunderstood as saying that modern ideas change with every shift in the nature of material conditions of existence and that the material form of a mode of production gives rise to institutional, legal, and political structures which imprison creative possibilities. In fact, a careful reading of materialist approaches to culture can promote an understanding of and appreciation for the power of capitalism as a social system whose strength lies in its capacity to mobilize the multiple imaginaries of all sectors of modern society on an ever-expanding scale. How does a scholar who wants to link urban culture to its historical, economic and spatial contexts avoid simplistic economic determinism? In other words, how can one link the material to the symbolic?

This book takes literary scholar Franco Moretti up on his recent invitation to do precisely this in his concise volume *Graphs, Maps, Trees. Abstract Models for a Literary History*. He asks a simple question about literary maps: "what do they do?" (2005: 35). He argues that they are a good way to prepare literary texts for analysis because they reduce the text to a few elements, enabling one to abstract from them the narrative flow, forcing one to construct an artificial object much like the text itself. "And with a little luck, these maps will be more than the sum of their parts: they will possess 'emerging' qualities, which were not visible at the lower level" (2005: 53). Moretti demonstrates how hidden patterns can be brought to the surface of a text when they are diagramed and their points seen in relation to one another. Moretti quotes D'Arcy Thompson when he says that "the form of an object is a 'diagram of forces'.... Deducing from the form of an object the forces that have been at work: that is the most elegant definition of what literary sociology should be" (2005: 57). In this way we will look at tangible relationships between urban social conflict and literary form – by charting maps and diagrams of fictional worlds where the real and imaginary coexist in varying and often elusive ways. What these diagrams and maps do is point out the various directions in which the process of urbanization forced the shape of the experience of modernity in Madrid.

If we take these considerations into account and locate the orientations of different power centers within an overall theory of a capitalist mode of production and try to identify relationships between the historical and geographical dynamics in Madrid, a close look at the urban context shows firm connections between the rules of capitalist accumulation and the ferment of social, political and cultural forms that arise in that place, in that time. Rather than a thing in itself, an independent object of inquiry, the modern city needs to be seen as an important element mediating and expressing wider social processes. What is imagined and what is real about the modern metropolis are both relative in that they depend on who is doing the imagining, who is doing the creating and who is interpreting the built environment. There is no one city but multiple perspectives and views of what is seemingly the same geographic location. Composed of competing ideologies, Madrid produced all manner of goods, material as well as cultural and ideological, new structures and new ideas that could only have been born of the urban. Sometimes men and women have power over their immediate surroundings, sometimes they do not. Sometimes they are conscious of how dominant ideologies influence their actions, sometimes they are not. The city and the culture of the city are both sites of power and are analyzed as such here. I end with the same thought with which I began this chapter: the urban planner, the architect, and the author all have to have some kind of model, some image, some abstract concept in mind before they construct their spatial imaginaries. Whether or not these spaces were created in the real world or not is secondary because they will continue to inform successive generations in a variety of ways.

CHAPTER II
Building Modern Madrid

Madrid has its own brand of popular musical revue called the *zarzuela* which is a place where language and social norms can be transgressed, where each character can reveal the truth as he or she sees it, and where many aspects of Spanish society are critiqued.[1] To understand how *madrileños* talked to one another about their city during the first years of its industrial, modern period one need look no further than to *La Gran Vía. Revista madrileña cómico-lírica, fantástico-callejera en un acto* by Federico Chueca and Joaquín Valverde, first presented in Madrid in 1886 and still immensely popular today. The plot provides an opportunity to show an array of characters in situations that are alternately realistic, fantastic and allegorical. In *La Gran Vía* the presence of the city goes from mere backdrop to being in the foreground of the action. Allegorical characters (Madrid streets, squares, alleys, the fountain in the

---

1. Gómez Amat's *Historia de la música española* traces the *zarzuela* back to the origins of Italian opera, but considers the genre uniquely Spanish and particularly *madrilenãn* (1984: 131-141). A *zarzuela* combines sung musical numbers with scenes that are spoken, unlike the opera. For a biography of Chueca and his working-class roots in Madrid see Gómez Amat (1984: 211-222).

Puerta del Sol, Electricity and Natural Gas, to name a few) as well as identifiable Madrid archetypes make way for a dramatic pretext consisting of a walk through central Madrid by the characters *El Paseante en Corte* [The Town Pedestrian] and *El Caballero de Gracia* [The Graceful Gentleman (also the name of a major street off the Gran Vía)] who await the birth of the *Gran Vía* to *Doña Municipalidad* [Madam Municipality]. *Amiguismo* (political "old-boy" networks) and *yernocracia* ("son-in-lawcracy") are decried, as is the lack of security for city dwellers caused by the rise of petty crime and the failure of the city policemen (the antiheroes of the story) to protect Madrid's citizens. Throughout *La Gran Vía* moral virtue belongs to the popular classes for whom the work was written.[2] The first dance number consists of maids and shop assistants who are joined by the city's cooks. The second demonstrates the approval and popularity of the *zarzuela* among the working class when a group of them flock *en masse* to the very theater where the actual performance is taking place. Close attention is paid to Madrid's chaotic development and the municipal government's lack of concern about the precarious situation of the outlying neighborhood of Prosperidad, for example, on the south side of town. The production focuses mainly on the construction of the Gran Vía, however, and the song lyrics contain complaints about the destruction of the fountain in the Puerta del Sol and document new technological advances such as electric light and refined oil leading to the disappearance of gas, as well as other urban changes brought about due to an increase in the use of electric trolleys.

In the last act, entitled "La Gran Vía," the audience is asked to assume that the Gran Vía is complete. On the stage it has become a symbol of "Science, Justice, Work and Virtue" protected by a Statue of Liberty holding a Spanish flag in her right hand. There is, however, a clear satirical note accompanying this optimistic vision of the future. The *Comadrón* [Doctor who assists in childbirth] announces the upcoming arrival of the grand avenue that he says will be born:

---

2. Parsons describes late nineteenth-century Madrid as a '*castizo* metropolis' and the *zarzuela* as an urban-based art form that established a series of idealized and distorted 'popular characters,' products of mostly middle-class writers (2003: 68-76).

Cuando llegue esta acción / un buen gobierno a tener
Y se cumpla en el Poder / lo dicho en la Oposición.
Cuando a ser ministro no / llegue nadie haciendo el bu,
Ni haya lo de 'vete tú / que quiero ponerme yo.'
Cuando no medre un ciruelo / a costa de los demás;
Cuando gane un sabio más / que Lagartijo y Frascuelo.
Cuando nadie invente acá / demagógicos excesos,
Y no se escapan más presos / ni roben iglesias ya;
Y la Hacienda Nacional / esté de recursos harta,
y no se pierde una carta / aunque lleve un dineral.
Y por fin ... cuando el destino / que a sernos contrario vino
Quiera mejorar el cielo .../ Y crie la rana pelo.

The *Paseante* asks:

¿Y ese día que yo espero / acaso ha llegado ya?

To which the *Comadrón* responds with

No tal: pero llegará.

The Chorus asks in unison:

¿Cuándo?

and the *Comadrón* dramatically sings:

¡El treinta de febrero!
Mas por mágico poder / hoy a vuestra fantasía
Puedo mostrar la Gran Vía / tal y como puede ser.

Comadrón
[This will happen / where there is a good government
And Power will achieve / what it said it would during its Campaign.
When one becomes Minister / one stops doing anything,
Not even the usual 'get out / so I can take power.'
When a wise man earns more / than [the bullfighters] Lagartijo and Frascuelo.
When no one here creates / excessive demagoguery,

And prisoners stop escaping / and no more churches are robbed;
And the National Treasury / has enough resources;
And no letter is misplaced / even if it is full of money.
And finally … when destiny / which came to vex us
Wants to improve the heavens … / when a frog grows hair.
Paseante:
And the day that I am waiting for / has it by any chance arrived yet?
Comadrón:
Not yet / but it will come.
Chorus:
When?
Comadrón:
On the thirtieth of February!
But through magic powers / I can show you the Gran Vía
As your fantasy today / such as it could be.]

In other words, the Gran Vía will be born when there is honor in power, when a wise man earns more than a bullfighter, when political life knows no corruption and when the treasury is full. Much of the enjoyment of the revue comes from witnessing the fleshing out of the modern utopian vision for the grand thoroughfare. There was a great distance between this fantasy and the actual expectations for the new space, however. This popular anticipation and fear of urban renewal both grew out of the dire need to solve serious urban problems, and the futuristic utopias that were often created by artists in Madrid at this time created an ongoing tension that thematically and structurally shaped urban cultural production in significant ways.

Madrid as Metropolis

La Gran Vía grew out of a rapidly-growing city at the turn of the century. Aggressive transformations in urban and social structures, mostly due to increasing industrialization, were causing major changes and bringing with them a new dynamism to the city. Immigration to the capital was both the result and the cause of many of these changes. During the first third of the twentieth century there was an enormous demographic change.[3] The population of the capital went from 539,835 to 952,832 between 1900 and 1930, while the peripheral small towns quadrupled their collective populations from 45,752 to 200,714 during the same period.[4] Soon there were more *madrileños* born outside than inside the city limits. By 1930, only 37 percent of Madrid's population had been born in the capital (Juliá/Ringrose/Segura 1995: 451).[5]

Economist Jordi Nadal is of the opinion that urban migration to the cities was high because of what he calls the "social costs" of the Spanish agricultural system that were taking their toll. Outdated, practically feudal rental contracts were enforced in Galicia and Catalonia. Low wages and seasonal unemployment in the areas of the large landed estates of Andalusia, Extremadura and La Mancha drove families away. The high instance of subsistence farming in regions like Old Castile and León and control by dominant economic groups guaranteed a rural repressive apparatus against which many Spaniards reacted (Nadal 1987: 54-60). Migration to South America was an effective safety valve for a time, and in some locations entire populations took advantage of this remedy. Approximately 1.5 million Spaniards left the country during the years 1904-1913, this number making up 8% of the entire population. During and after World War I, however, when this migratory outlet was closed off, increasingly urban social tensions began to boil over (Nadal 1984: 193-226).

A quick look at the occupational makeup of Madrid's rapidly growing population in 1930 suggests that almost all of the people coming to Madrid at this time were young professionals, servants, construction

---

3. From the beginning of the century until 1930, the province of Madrid received 449,493 immigrants: 72,161 in the first decade, 158,682 in the second and 219,650 in the third (Juliá 1995: 453).

4. As late as 1931, at the outbreak of the Second Republic in April of 1931, 43 percent of the Spanish population was still employed in the agricultural sector, 34 percent in the industrial and 18 in the service sector. The average life expectancy was 51. This would jump to 77 by 1990 (Nadal 1984: 2).

5. See Tuñón de Lara's *Medio siglo* for a detailed overview of the social consequences of this demographic situation.

workers or clerks. Major construction companies such as Agromán,
Fierro and Fomento hired thousands of men to work on public projects. More were needed to work in factories such as El Águila (producing beer), Standard Eléctrica (electricity), Perfumería Gal (soap and
perfumes), Rivadeneyra (in publishing), Compañía Metropolitano
(construction) and Gas Madrid (natural gas) (Juliá/Ringrose/Segura
1995: 456). It is during this period that the Spanish urban working
class was formed.

Manpower was in high demand because in addition to industrialization, the city was undergoing major infrastructural and architectural changes between 1900 and 1936. From the beginning of the
century, for example, the Paseo del Prado ennobled itself with the construction of Antonio Palacios's Palacio de Comunicaciones in the Plaza
de Cibeles. French and British capital helped construct the Plaza de
Neptuno and the Ritz and Palace Hotels. The major project, though,
the one that received the most sustained attention of the government,
private investors and of the city's citizens, was the construction of the
Gran Vía. It would take almost fifty years, but there would eventually
be a modern boulevard running from Cibeles to the Plaza de España,
linking the Salamanca and Arguelles neighborhoods. From those who
designed the neo-baroque, highly-decorated buildings of the beginning of the century to the "moderns" who built the rationalist buildings of the late twenties and early thirties, the architects who came to
work on the great buildings of the Gran Vía (people like Jules and Raymond Fevrier, Secundino Ugalde Zuazo, Pedro Muguruza Otaño and
Teodoro Anasagasti) had the chance to experiment with new building
techniques and styles.

The construction of the Gran Vía has a long history. It begins in
1898, when the Mayor of Madrid, the Conde de Romanones, proposed a project to build a "gran vía" which would help to relieve congestion in the city, in a similar way to the Haussmann Avenue in Paris
during the Second Empire. The "Haussmannization" of modern nineteenth-century cities, as chronicled in the work of Walter Benjamin,
was contrived by Napoleon and his prefect of the Seine, Baron Georges
Haussmann, to modernize Paris's infrastructure, creating sweeping

boulevards, a new sewer system, and a reconstructed central market.[6] Urban historians agree that the Gran Vía, while undoubtedly inspired by the spirit of Haussmann's Second Empire project, was a significantly more modest affair.[7]

Construction began in earnest in 1910, with Alfonso XIII making the first symbolic blows with a pick-axe from the luxury of carpeted scaffolding. Approximately 311 buildings, mostly residential, were destroyed to make way for the construction of the Gran Vía (Cortizo/Sobrino 1997: xx). (*Fig. 2.1*) What replaced them were much grander buildings devoted either to leisure or to the functions of an increasingly capitalist state bureaucracy. The creation of new institutions seemed to be going on at the very same time as the buildings that housed them. The Círculo de la Unión Industrial y Mercantil and the Casino Militar housed business and military interests; the great warehouses Madrid-París and Casa Matesanz aided in the distribution of goods in the central urban area; the Círculo de Bellas Artes, the Palacio de la Música and the movie theaters Callao and Capitol helped further public interest in a nascent film industry; the Telefónica building was the home of a quickly-growing communications empire. In terms of transportation, the most important development was brought to fruition by the engineer Miguel Otamendi who presented the plans for the first underground railway line, whose construction began in 1917. Funded with capital from the Banco de Vizcaya and King Alfonso XIII, Cuatro Caminos and the Puerta del Sol were linked by underground rail in 1919, and Atocha another two years later (Juliá 1995: 487).

---

6. Pinkney argues that Haussmannization was also an important act of social control in that the boulevards destroyed working-class enclaves, impeded the building of barricades and facilitated the deployment of troops in case of insurrection. It is important to note that these controversial changes made a formerly labyrinthine geography more legible, orienting Paris towards greater visibility.

7. As early as 1929, the popular press in Madrid featured articles and editorials complaining that the Gran Vía was too narrow to accommodate the demands of foot and automobile traffic. In response, the Castellana extension would be significantly wider than the Gran Vía (see Sambricio 2003: 139-142).

The neighborhoods of Atocha and Cuatro Caminos were quite another story, however. It was in these neighborhoods that the effects of
the other side of the industrial boom could be felt. These parts of town
grew quickly and chaotically, with no planning whatsoever. It is estimated that about 30 percent of Cuatro Caminos consisted of squatters
in 1930 (Juliá 1995: 458). (*Fig. 2.2*) The labor necessary to build
Madrid's new projects was housed here, in shacks called *chabolas* constructed around the edges of Madrid. In the north there were Cuatro
Caminos and Tetuán; in the East, Prosperidad and Guindalera; in the
Southeast, the underdeveloped neighborhood of the Puente de Vallecas
that eventually extended all the way to the town of Vallecas; in the
South, Toledo, San Isidro and Carabanchel. Much of Madrid's recently-
arrived population lived in these areas linked by unpaved roads and suf-
fered in substandard living conditions with insufficient plumbing, no
waste disposal, no electricity and few if any municipal services.

The First Attempts to Plan the Modern City

Not just the size and demographics but the shape of Madrid changed
drastically during the first three decades of the twentieth century. New
neighborhoods were built, mostly on the edges of the city, and some
parts of the medieval *casco antiguo* were renovated, sometimes quite
dramatically. The men who made the decisions as to where and when
to invest money in the reshaping of the city belonged to a brand-new
discipline: urban planning. The concept of urban planning was born towards the end of the nineteenth century, part of a concerted effort to design – using rational social and scientific theories – an alternative to the
horrific chaos of the nineteenth-century city, what Peter Hall has called
"The City of Dreadful Night" in the title of one of the chapters of his
work *Cities of Tomorrow* (1988). Alternatives were desperately needed
in Madrid, which was suffering from many of the same problems as the
cities of the rest of Europe.

The city as the site of industrialization throughout Europe was a
place of decay, poverty, social malaise and civil unrest. It was in the best
interest of governments to develop ways of controlling their increasingly

urban inhabitants. According to Hall in *Cities of Tomorrow*, twentieth-century urban planners were concerned not just with rehabilitating an existing city center but with developing the region immediately surrounding the city, taking each urban region's ecology and particular culture into consideration (1988: 1-13). The work of urban planners has often involved the restructuring of not just one region, but the relationships between regions. As a consequence, one chief topic of interest in urban planning has always been the relationship between the spreading megalopolis and the depopulating countryside. As well as taking into account the built environment of a region, the success of these plans relies on complementary regional and national economic infrastructures built on healthy social and political development. From the start, one can see that for these plans to go into effect as intended, long-term commitments to policies needed to be implemented on the national, regional and local levels. Unfortunately, twentieth-century Spain (like almost every other European country, for that matter) was never able to enjoy these ideal circumstances.[8]

The key concepts of the incipient planning movement that would eventually have an impact on Spanish urban planners belong to British names like Howard, Unwin, Parker Abercrombie and Osborne, as well as American names such as Geddes, Mumford, Stein, MacKaye and Chase. With the notable exception of the Ciudad Lineal of Arturo Soria, the most influential concepts of urban planning in the first part of the century are undeniably Anglo-Saxon. London led the world in this kind of urban thinking, though to do so it imported American transportation technologies and entrepreneurship. Hall divides twentieth-century philosophies of urban planning into four categories, some of which at one time or another overlap. They are: 1) the garden-city concept of Ebenezer Howard; 2) the regional city developed by Geddes and later Lewis Mumford, Clarence Stein and Henry Wright

---

8. Hall repeatedly acknowledges the shortcoming of planning and urban theory but maintains hope in the possibilities of his discipline. 'Most of these ideas, though bereft of all possibility of realization when first conceived, were essentially the product of activists, of the doers of this world' (1988: 10).

of the Regional Planning Association of America; 3) the monumental tradition of city planning; and 4) the dramatic high-rise and highway city of Le Corbusier. Hall develops the history of urban planning around the premise that almost all of the visions of these men (Le Corbusier being the notable exception) stemmed from the founding principles of the Anarchist movement (1988: 3-9, 1988: 143-144). David Goodway, cognizant of the fact that there are many different types of anarchy and anarchists, provides a good general working definition of the movement.

> Anarchists have traditionally identified the major social, economic, and political problems as consisting of capitalism, inequality (including the domination of women by men), sexual repression, militarism, war, authority and the state.... Positively, what anarchists advocate are egalitarianism, co-operation (mutual aid), workers' control (self-management), individualism, freedom, and complete decentralization (organization from the bottom up). As means, they propose direct action (spontaneity) and direct democracy (wherever possible, for they are ultra-democrats, supporting delegation against representation). (1989: 8-9)

If one understands historical anarchy in this way, one can see that some commonalities exist between the first urban planners and the anarchist movement because the planners wanted much more than to create new built forms. They envisioned an alternative society, neither capitalistic nor bureaucratic-socialistic: a society based on voluntary cooperation among men and women, working and living in self-governing commonwealths. Unfortunately, "when the time came at last for their ideas to be translated into bricks and mortar, the irony was that—more often than not—this happened through the agency of state bureaucracies, which they [the planners] hated" (Hall 1988: 3). Their ideas were often so diluted that the end results went so far as to bring about a subsequent disillusionment with the idea of planning itself in the second half of the twentieth century. Not surprisingly, this is also the fate of some of the best plans of Spanish urban developers in Madrid during the first third of the century.

One of the responses to the problems of the Victorian city was that of Ebenezer Howard, whose ideas were formulated and articulated over the period of 1880-98. He proposed to solve the problem of the centralized industrial city by exporting a large number of the city's citizens and jobs to new, self-contained constellations of towns built in the open countryside, far from the slums and the smoke and most importantly, the overblown land values of the giant city. This model would be called by subsequent students and planners the Garden City. These ideas were eventually adapted in the form of either pure dormitory suburbs (the antithesis of what Howard stood for), to utopian schemes to depopulate the great cities and recolonize the countryside.

Hall considers Patrick Geddes's concept of the Regional City the second response to the urban problems of the nineteenth century. It takes Howard's central theme much further, conceptually and geographically. Geddes's response to the sordid congestion of the giant city is a vast program of regional planning, within which each subregional part would be harmoniously developed on the basis of its own natural resources, with respect to principles of ecological balance and resource renewal. Cities, in Geddes's scheme of things, should become subordinate to the region. Old cities and new towns grow as necessary parts of the regional scheme. This concept would have a great influence on New Deal planners in the United States, most notably Rexford Tugwell, and form the founding vision of the Regional Planning Association of America. Hall says of the Regional City that in its pure form "it offered so much but in the end, it was to offer much less" (1988: 141).

The Greek-inspired monumental tradition was championed by the likes of master planners such as Georges-Eugène Haussman in Paris and Ildefonso Cerdá in Barcelona in the late nineteenth century, and later by Fascist urban planners in Germany, Italy and Franco's Spain. Hall calls it "the handmaiden of civic pride allied to commercial boosterism in America" (1988: 9). Oblivious to wider social concerns, its purpose was to symbolize totalitarian power, pomp and prestige. Tangentially related to both the Garden City and the monumental-city concepts of urban planning, the vision of the Swiss-born French architect-planner Le Corbusier proposed that the greatest evil of the modern city was its density and that the remedy, perversely, was to increase that density. Le Corbusier's solution, whereby the master-planner would demolish the entire existing city and replace it with a series

of high-rise buildings in a park, rarely found favor in its pure form
(Hall 1988: 14). All of these above-mentioned promises of continual
progress and endless improvement through the design of urban space
that make up the history of urban planning have had an impact on
Madrid's modern built environment. It is one of the myths of modernity, though, that any one of these plans has been successful in the
long term. Almost from the very beginning of the twentieth century
there was a steady stream of able, articulate Spanish engineers and architects who began their careers in Madrid after having studied the
latest urban planning techniques and concepts in Britain, Germany
and the United States. Many of these highly-skilled young professionals found jobs in city government and published articles in important architecture and design magazines.

Madrid's Urban Planning, 1900 – 1936

Informed by the British and American urban planners mentioned above,
Spanish architects and engineers realized that they needed to reconsider the very idea of what a city was. Those who thought of the long
term, of the bigger picture, seemed to think that a lack of affordable
housing for all was every modern city's biggest problem. The problem
was thought solvable by a reevaluation of the role of the land located
outside of the city limits and the construction of small, independent
or semi-independent municipalities in these areas. They thought that
no matter how many important roadways were made to guarantee
easier transportation routes within the city, no matter how many buildings were built, that looking towards orderly and even expansion on the
outskirts of the city was the only way to relieve the population density
and raise the standard of living for the city's inhabitants. Unfortunately, this kind of thinking, over time, resulted in a sharp increase in
the price of the land on the very edge of the developed city, which
made an impossibility of the true Garden City. No city government
had the strength to withstand the loss of support of important land-
holders who owned the land on the immediate outskirts of town (Sambricio 1999: 43).

Many of Madrid's first urban planners were idealistic, political progressives who fought for the acceptance of their plans because they thought of their work as an important step in the reordering of society, as a revolution from above. Much to their dismay, even compromised versions of their urban visions were never implemented due to lack of private and/or state capital. The pure, theoretical vision of the Regional Plan, where the countryside and industrial center were developed and integrated for the greater good of both and for the benefit of all classes, was a utopia never achieved either in or outside of Spain. Amós Salvador, an influential urban planner who had studied and attended the most important British planning school in London and regularly attended the conferences of the Town Planning Association of England as early as 1909, considered himself a follower of the Garden City plan but saw that the pure model was unfeasible. In his words "no hay que oponer la ciudad millonaria a la ciudad-jardín, puesto que los nuevos proyectos están anexionando suburbios-jardín a grandes ciudades" [the millionaire's city does not have to be opposed to the Garden City since the new projects are annexing Garden Cities to the suburban areas] (quoted in Sambricio 1984: 27).

In Spain the definition of the Garden City itself comes to mean something quite different from what Ebenezer Howard intended. Teodoro de Anaragasti is fully aware of this when he asks: "¿Qué es la ciudad-jardín? ¿Cómo debemos definirla? ... ¿Será aquella en que cada casa está rodeada de grandes espacios libres, de verdor de un recinto mayor que el ocupado por la edificación? Este fue el concepto más sencillo, el de la casa-jardín más que el de ciudad-jardín" [What is the Garden City? How should we define it? Should it be the house surrounded by large, green, open spaces greater in size than the building itself? This is the simplest concept, more Garden House than Garden City] (quoted in Sambricio 1999: 28). In Spain the small, short-term project would always be undertaken instead of the far-sighted regional plan. Maure Rubio states the key problem:

> Las corrientes arquitectónicas descuidaron casi por completo el problema de las masas humanas en expansión en los barrios pobres de la periferia, que surgían más por conveniencia de los intereses privados que

por una lógica respuesta a necesidades sociales... Sólo más tarde, dema-
siado tarde, los arquitectos se dan cuenta de la importancia formativa de
estos barrios y del error de no haberlos concebido en función de la nueva
estructura de la ciudad. (1986: 139)

> [Architectural trends paid almost no attention to the human crowds
> that were occupying the neighborhoods in the outlying areas, the neigh-
> borhoods that existed more for the convenience of private interests than as
> a logical response to social needs.... Only later, too late, did the architects
> realize the formative significance of these neighborhoods and the mistake of
> not having incorporated them into the new structure of the city.]

Any and all urban restructuring during this politically and economically unstable time was admittedly ambitious and idealistic. The chief
factor impeding the implementation of these plans was the lack of cooperation between government law-making bodies (municipal, regional
and national) and private construction. It was only later, with the plans
of men like Secundino Zuazo and Indalecio Prieto, who, as heads of
government agencies and insiders in the world of commerce, that any
of the plans accepted by Spanish governing bodies came to fruition.
The policies of Zuazo and Prieto, as we will see, provided jobs for a
needy workforce during the Second Republic, much like the New Deal
and the WPA did a few years later in the United States. Their plans for
Madrid's development, however, provided no housing for those living
in substandard conditions in Madrid's peripheral zones and no increased access to transportation, communication or other social services
for the majority of Madrid's citizens. The periphery of Madrid, always
the city's greatest tragedy and planning concern, continued to be developed with neither a sense of order nor a concept of how it could
work with other regions and the urban center in a humane way.

A look at the major plans for urban development proposed between
1909 and 1936 in Madrid leads to several conclusions. One is that for
the reasons outlined above, they were well meaning, even at times politically and socially progressive, but ultimately untenable because they
were not based on a knowledge of capital flow in modern industrial society. Another is that there was no great ideological difference in the
plans accepted for implementation during the dictatorship of Primo de

Rivera and the Second Republic. What becomes clear is that Madrid during this period becomes more and more structured around capital and that space is created in the image of capital regardless of which leader or party held the reins of political power.

Pedro Núñez Garcés presented a major plan to the Madrid City Council in 1909. Unlike previous plans, it included specific instructions on how to deal with the growing problem of the neighborhoods forming on the edges of the city. In his words:

[d]ebemos solicitar que el Ayuntamiento ordene la formación de un verdadero plan de urbanización en las zonas periféricas de Madrid, proponiéndolas en relación con el ensanche del casco interior y tratando de crear para el futuro una ciudad instrumento de progreso material y de cultura, cómoda, salubre y bella. Un plan de urbanización no puede descender a proyectar casa por casa. Sólo el iniciar tal idea es prueba de idiotez. Pero un buen plan de urbanización no puede dejar de prever: 1) el trazado de grandes vías de comunicación y transporte (ferrocarriles y tranvías); 2) la posición de las estaciones de estas líneas; 3) el recorrido de las conducciones de agua, energía eléctrica, gas, etc.; 4) la distribución del conjunto del urbe en ciudades semi-independientes en distritos de carácter diferente, en barrios distintos; y 5) la interpolación de jardines, parques, campos de juego y bosques. (quoted in Sambricio 1999: 20)

[we should ask the city to call for the formation of a true urban plan for the peripheral zones of Madrid, taking into account their relationship to the historical urban center and trying to create a city that is instrumental to a future of material progress, culture, comfort, health and beauty. An urban plan cannot focus on building house by house. To even begin at that scale is idiotic. But a good urban plan cannot help but promote: 1) the design of major routes of communication and transportation (trains and railways); 2) the positioning of stations along these railways; 3) the running of water, electric and gas lines; 4) dividing the entire city into semi-independent cities that have their own character, their own types of neighborhoods; and 5) the placement of intermittent parks, playgrounds and other types of shaded areas.]

This plan was approved by the city council but quickly abandoned. Interested parties of urban landowners included a powerful class of investors that had been strengthened by Spain's economic success in no small part due its neutrality during the First World War. Sambricio points out that this class

> entendía el casco interior y el ensanche como lugar de producción de ri-
> quezas y que definía las grandes vías como lugares de producción de ideo-
> logía. La burguesía surgida tras la guerra mundial ve, en la ordenación del
> suelo, un primer negocio y, en este sentido, fomentará y aplaudirá cual-
> quier operación que cree suelo urbano. (1999: 21)

> [understood the historical city center and its extension as a place of wealth
> production that defined the great boulevards as places where ideology was
> produced. The middle class that came out of the First World War made
> the remaking of that area its most important business and, in this sense,
> invested in and applauded any operation that created a profit.]

In essence, this is why money poured into the radical reformation of the Gran Vía, at the expense of almost all other neighborhoods.

In the 1920s Spanish urban planners began to look more to the United States for ideas on how to control and order a rapidly-growing metropolis. This is unlike what was happening in Barcelona, which starts to model itself after what was then seen as the successful zoning and redevelopment of Berlin (Hughes 1991: 380-385). Implicit in the Salaberry Expansion Plan of 1923 is a rejection of some aspects of the previously-mentioned Núñez Garcés Plan. Carlos Alberto Salaberry was of the opinion that the previous plan was too old-fashioned, rigid and did not take into account the topographic reality of the hilly regions surrounding Madrid. He also felt that it did not respond to the city's natural inclination in previous years to develop from north to south, from Fuencarral, Chamartín and Ciudad Lineal in the north to Vallecas and Carabanchel in the south. Núñez Garcés's plan seemed to ignore already existing working-class communities that had sprung up in Cuatro Caminos, Puente de Vallecas, and all along the Carabanchel and Andalucía routes out of town. Paradoxically, there seemed by the 1920s to be an entirely unplanned growth in well-to-do, privately-funded housing that could fit the Garden City model around Chamartín, the Hipódromo and the Aragón highway that needed to be taken into account. Núñez Garcés's plan said nothing about how to incorporate these communities into the big picture. He had also failed to leave a clearly-defined space for an industrial region. The Salaberry Plan, though, still stuck resolutely to Ebenezer Howard's concept of the Garden City, often citing Howard's Housing and Town Planning Act of 1909. Salaberry wanted to be more sensitive and realistic about working within the urban situation as it existed. Like the Núñez plan, though, it was enthusiastically accepted, and then quickly abandoned for the same reasons as that of its predecessor (Sambricio 1984: 20-21).

In 1925 projects working towards a Regional Plan for Madrid came to a halt. One reason was that Primo de Rivera was in power and his government had an even closer relationship with the land-owning bourgeoisie than had the previous government. The more pressing reason was that after so many failures, planners began to seek new solutions to old problems. Laws were passed (the Leyes de Casas Baratas [Affordable Housing Laws] in 1924 and 1926) to mandate the immediate construction of inexpensive housing and to help ease unemployment in the process. Very little actual building took place, however, due in large part to the fact that between 1917 and 1923 the price of building materials had skyrocketed: bricks 500%, iron 500% and plaster 300%, due to the global economic crisis (Fernández Polanco 1994: 55-58). Some large apartment-like housing units called *bloques* were constructed in parts of town where land was inexpensive and social services were non-existent. When houses went up in good, accessible parts of town intended for those with low incomes, they were ultimately purchased by the middle and upper-middle classes.

1924 is an important year for Spanish urban planners in a theoretical sense, however. The Primer Congreso Nacional de Urbanismo [First National Urban Congress] was held. The ideas presented there about planning in Spain drew from and further developed what was going on in Britain. At this time the international urban planning community was keenly interested in the ideas of two Englishmen, Unwin and Abercrombie, disciples of Howard, who still adhered to the possibility and the necessity of achieving not just a small-scale urban rehabilitation but a full-scale Regional Plan. They wanted to avoid having to transport masses of workers between their homes and their places of work and attempted to plan cities where people worked close to home, at a distance from the urban center. Núñez Garcés, inspired by these slightly revised theories of planning in 1924 and then again in 1926 presented his British-inspired Regional Plan to the Madrid City Council. This time he called attention to eight aspects that need to be included in the construction of the new region:

> 1) investigación física: geología, nivel, vientos, lluvias, vegetación; 2) desarrollo histórico; 3) comercio e industria: tendencias de centralización o descentralización; 4) población y viviendas: densidades, condiciones de casas; 5) sanidad: comparación de las condiciones sanitarias y determinación de los requisitos indispensables; 6) medios de comunicación: métodos diferentes, su consideración distinto de lo local; 7) espacios libres: estudio de los parques existentes y determinación de los terrenos susceptibles de ser destinados a este fin; 8) aspectos generales: utilización del terreno como base de información general, saneamiento natural que demuestra las tendencias generales del desarrollo y sumario de los diferentes aspectos de la investigación. (quoted in Sambricio 1984: 153)

> [1] physical research: geology, altitude, wind, rain, vegetation; 2) historic development; 3) commerce and industry: tendencies towards centralization or decentralization; 4) population and housing: density, the conditions of housing; 5) sanitation: the comparison of health conditions and the determination of useful standards; 6) means of communication: different methods, their distance from housing; 7) open space: the study of existing parks and determining which areas can be used as parks in the future; 8) general aspects: overall land use, health issues and their relationship to development and a summary of the varied aspects of the investigation.]

Incredibly, the plans of 1924 and 1926 also passed, but this would be the last time for many decades that anyone would seriously promote the Regional Plan, the Garden City or anything that resembled the work of the British urban theorists. For all of those involved in actually putting up capital, passing zoning laws and building telephone lines and railroads, these plans were nothing but utopian dreams and no way to imagine the city of the future. The members of the City Council as well as the Unión Patriótica (the political party in power) had other interests: maintaining and strengthening an already-existing economic order based on the appropriation of rents derived from increasing land values. Any radical expansion or construction of satellite cities threatened their hold on power.

By 1929 urban problems in Madrid were growing even more acute. Population growth was still soaring. Dangerous, unsanitary, impromptu housing continued to go up on all sides of the city. The dictatorship of Primo de Rivera had no control over the situation and political unrest was getting out of hand. The Gabinete de Estudios Urbanos [Urban Studies Cabinet] (GEU) decided to try something different. They announced an open competition, a call for projects to save the city called the Anteproyecto para la Urbanización y Extensión de Madrid "para tratarse de análisis del extrarradio, extensión y reformas interiores, como un plan de conjunto" [Preliminary Plan for the Urbanization and Extensión of Madrid "in order to deal with the outlying areas, the extension and interior reforms as a whole] (Sambricio 1984: 69). The participants were given a strict set of guidelines and told to come up with creative solutions to the city's problems. All work turned over to the city would then be the property of the GEU.

Twelve plans were submitted. Tellingly, no clear winner was officially declared because no one single plan was able to comply with all of the regulations and rules established beforehand. Six were selected as being worthy of serious consideration, however. The team of Ularqui and Czekelius, full of Corbusian fervor, proposed the immediate removal of much of the *casco antiguo* so tall high-rise buildings could house the masses. Thankfully, this plan was disregarded. The plan of the team of Secundino Zuazo and the German architect Otto Jensen was chosen. What is surprising is that, unlike other plans, this one (which was never officially approved by the City Council) ended up being implemented on a grand scale. Ironically, Zuazo's conception of the city was radically different from any that came before in that it was rooted in history and tradition. "Todo ... debe llevarse a cumplimiento de acuerdo con la obra tradicional de Madrid, sin destruir sus líneas fundamentales y sus módulos característicos sin borrar su tradición urbanística y sí favoreciéndola, confirmándola y mejorándola" [Everything ... should be accomplished in a way that is consistent with traditional

Madrid, without destroying her fundamental lines and characteristic modules, without erasing her urban traditions but featuring them, confirming them and improving them] (quoted in Sambricio 1984: 71). He was one of the first urban planners in Spain truly familiar with the workings of land speculation and capital investment. From the very beginning he wanted to put a halt to the exodus of the population to the periphery, and sought to redevelop the city center. His plans were successful in no small part because they required the development of every last meter of the highest-priced land in the city, so there was no shortage of private funding to be found. Best of all, no zoning laws would have to be changed (Sambricio/Maure 1984: 158-160).

The problem with this plan is self-evident, however. It places power not in the hands of a government body interested in long-term goals but in the hands of the land-owning class interested in making money on their immediate investments. Because Zuazo did not believe the city should grow in concentric circles, it grew in a northern direction, chiefly through the extension of the Castellana. His Nuevos Ministerios became an important part of that extension (Sambricio/Maure 1984:139-160). Accompanying and complementing the extension of this area (which became a home for the wealthier classes) two other areas were developed: El Pardo to the northwest and Chamartín to the northeast. Between El Pardo and Chamartín de la Rosa a new working-class neighborhood was constructed. Tetuán was also completely adapted to low-income housing.

Zuazo's plan was not implemented right away, however. Neither was it implemented in full. It would take on more of a shape later on during Franco's regime. Political upheaval got in the way of any serious urban development. In 1931, only four months after the Second Republic came to power, a team of architects, engineers, administrators and urban planners came up with the Plan General de la Red Viaria Principal de la Extensión de Madrid y de Alineaciones y Rasantes de la Zona del Extrarradio [General Plan for the Principal Train Lines of the Extension of Madrid and the Alignment of the Outlying Zones] (Sambricio/Maure 1984: 175). It is with this plan that the municipal government began to think more seriously about its role as the nation's capital. The ideological climate had shifted. Manuel Lorite, in charge of the Republic's Oficina de Urbanismo Municipal [Office of Municipal Urbanism], criticized the Zuazo Plan, saying it was out of date and backward:

> los grupos actuales son diametralmente opuestos, dado que el mejora-miento de vida de esas clases sociales—la obrera y la media—y su parti-cipación directa en el Gobierno del país imponen nuevas normas y nuevas ordenanzas de ciudad…. Zuazo y Jansen han tenido su momento y tu-vieron su razón de ser en un régimen de supremacia capitalista, en que zonas residenciales eran una manifestación de poder y riqueza necesarios a su desarrollo. (quoted in Sambricio 2003: 81)

> [the groups at the moment are diametrically opposed, since the improve-ment of the lives of those social classes – the working class and the mid-dle class – and their direct participation in the country's government demand new norms and new urban ordinances…. Zuazo and Jansen have had their moment and have served their purpose in a regime of capitalist supremacy, in which the residential areas were a show of power and wealth necessary for their development.]

The plan of 1931 was again based on the Regional Plan. Never before had a group of such skilled Spanish urban planners worked together to renovate Madrid. This time around, the men responsible for drawing up the plan devoted most of their work to organizing a government agency able to work through and with all of the other agencies necessary to bring about such a huge undertaking. Unfortunately, the plan was still too short-sighted in that it ignored the already-existing outlying communities that by now had grown to be quite large. Chamartín de la Rosa had a population of 36,000 people. Vicálvaro and Canillejas each had 10,000, Pozuelo de Alarcón 3,000, and Carabanchel Alto y Bajo together almost 33,000. These communities alone made up a fifth of the total population of the city of Madrid (Juliá 1995: 479).

There was another serious problem with this plan, this time an overtly political one. The Socialist Party (PSOE) was against anything that did not immediately solve the worker's housing problem so they supported any private investor willing to put up huge *bloques* – the large, tall housing blocks on the edges of town. They were constructed quickly because they brought profits to the landowners since the land was at a premium. This structurally inferior housing turned these spaces into miserable, crime-infested, unhygienic areas far from the city center. Once again, a plan for urban development and restructuring was unsuccessful because it was based on an untried, imported concept that ignored the history and tradition of the city. The political Left, thinking of short-term problems, could not see beyond the existing structure of the city. For these reasons political reformists and urban planners in early twentieth-century Madrid were unable to make significant large-scale changes to their modern urban environment.

With Indalecio Prieto as Minister of Public Works, however, there was progress in some areas. He was articulate, knowledgeable and made an effort to inform *madrileños* of the plans being made for their city through the popular press. (*Fig. 2.3*) Because of his experience as Treasury Minister in the first two years of the Second Republic, he was aware of the economic situations of both the country as a whole and of Madrid in particular, and had ideas about how to secure and maintain investment in major projects.

Prieto asked Zuazo to help implement his new plan, in part because of his experience but also because the new plan would incorporate most of the changes to the structure of the railroad originally formulated by Zuazo. The inclusion of Zuazo in the group slated to reorganize the city pleased land owners and developers who were sure he would keep their interests in mind. The first phase of the plan, called the Plan Comarcal, involved bringing the train rails to towns along the Madrid/Avila line, and to places such as Aravaca, Pozuelo, Las Rozas, Torrelodones and El Escorial. Another line circumvented the city, linking San Sebastián de los Reyes, Colmenar Viejo, San Agustín de Guadalix, Manzanares del Real, Miraflores de la Sierra, and Valdemoro (Sambricio 2003: 76). The final stage of railroad development was to link these northern lines to the Madrid-Burgos line, thus uniting all the lines running north and south. Some of these towns became places of residence. Some would soon become industrial centers in themselves. Consequently, satellite cities were beginning to be formed in a controlled manner. There was little attention to design and the development in these areas was chaotic and subject to the individual battles of land developers with their own interests at heart, but nonetheless there was some degree of municipal planning and state control that occurred. People started to receive the social services they needed to live healthier lives.

Meanwhile, the bourgeoisie within the city were pleased with the new Nuevos Ministerios buildings and the extension of the Castellana into new centers of power and a place to live. The Nuevos Ministerios were built in the monumental, Greek-inspired style that spoke to those who sought comfort in the trappings of strong government. Of course, this monumental façade could not hide the fact that the government was remarkably unstable and Zuazo's unfinished project was halted at the outbreak of the Civil War. Since Zuazo was not looked upon kindly by the Franco regime because of his participation in the Second Republic, his project would be taken over, completed and greatly changed by a group of pro-Nationalist architects (Urrutia 1997: 230-240).

As is demonstrated repeatedly above, urban planning is inevitably tied to capital. It requires a great amount of money to change a neighborhood, put in a subway line or construct a building. Even the construction of a private home is the result of a major alignment of politics, art and capital. In Spain, like most other places, large buildings built for business, government, leisure or residential purposes require funding from business interests seeking a return on their investment. There were two closely related groups of architects formed in Spain in 1925 who responded to these challenges, the national GATEPAC (Grupo de Artistas y Técnicos Españoles para el Progreso de la Arquitectura Contemporánea) [Group of Spanish Artists and Technicians for the Progress of Contemporary Architecture] and the Catalan GATCPAC (Grupo de Artistas y Técnicos Catalanes para el Progreso de la Arquitectura Catalana) [Group of Catalan Artists and Technicians for the Progress of Catalan Architecture]. Their central philosophies are chronicled in the visually striking journal *AC* (*Documentos de Actividad Contemporánea*) (Bohigas 1998: 18-24, Urrutia 1992: 333-334). Both groups were fully cognizant of the difficulties of constructing good buildings in an urban environment and sought to promote a style of architecture that was more functional and rational than that of the past. Madrid has its share of these avant-garde structures, although there are many more in Barcelona because the Socialist politicians funded Catalan architects deeply involved in the GATEPAC/Modernist movement whereas architects in Madrid enthusiastic about this type of building and design usually resorted to the support of private donors (San Antonio 1996: 287-299).

This style of architecture and design has its corollary in what Lefebvre in his collection of essays *The Production of Space* describes as a moment of the emergence of an awareness of urban space and its production in the historic role of the Bauhaus.[9] After World War I this type of architecture did more than just supply a new perspective on space. Rational architecture developed a new and global conception of space. Lefebvre is of the opinion that it is the first rational articulation of the link between industrialization, work and the dwelling place (1991: 183-185). It was seen as both rational and revolutionary (although with hindsight we see that it was tailor-made for the state, both capitalist and socialist). The Bauhaus, Art Deco and the avant-gardes of this period understood that objects could not be created independently of each other in space without taking into account their relationship to the whole (Cooper 2004: 47-56). With the Bauhaus as with much of the avant-garde, the artist is concerned not with objects in space but in the concept of space itself. If the unfortunate result of

---

9. The Bauhaus was a German architectural and design institute founded in 1919. When it was closed down by the Nazis in 1933 it had moved three times and produced few graduates. Naylor points out that '[i]n order to effect the transition from nineteenth-century to twentieth-century attitudes, Gropius enlisted the help of avant-garde artists such as Feininger, Klee, Kandinsky and Moholy-Nagy; it was their function to create and stimulate the creative process; and their attitudes to shape, color, space and form had a profound influence on the Bauhaus' (1986: 7). The Bauhaus sought to use all of its resources: technical, scientific, intellectual and aesthetic, to create nothing less than an environment that would satisfy mankind's spiritual as well as material needs. For a detailed description of the Bauhaus, see Dearstyne's *Inside the Bauhaus* (1986) about his experience as a student there.

the Bauhaus was homogenous and monotonous architecture of the
state (capitalist or socialist), Lefebvre argues, this proves once again
that there is such a thing as a space characteristic of capitalism. Neither
the avant-garde nor professedly liberal governments can deny the all-
permeating influence of capital. Harvey puts it this way:

> [i]n much of contemporary architecture the city is a thing that can be
> engineered successfully in such a way as to control, contain, modify or en-
> hance social processes. In the nineteenth century Olmstead, Geddes,
> Howard, Burnham, Sitte, Wagner, Unwin, all reduced the problem of intri-
> cate social processes to a matter of finding the right spatial form. And in this
> they set the 'Utopic' twentieth-century tone for either a mechanistic ap-
> proach to urban form, as in the case of Le Corbusier, or the more organic
> approach of Frank Lloyd Wright. The difficulty with so-called 'high mod-
> ernism' and the city was not its 'totalizing vision' but its persistent habit of
> privileging things and spatial forms over social processes. (1996: 418-419)

With hindsight, historians can trace over the course of the nineteenth
and twentieth centuries the gradual disenchantment of architects and
urban planners with what Harvey calls here the "mechanistic approach
to urban form" in Spain and elsewhere. The construction of the urban
utopias imagined by the engineers and planners who had the power to
shape urban space by and large never came to fruition. But their plans,
desires and ideas about shaping space deserve careful scrutiny. Fictions
in their own right, the ideal spaces they imagined are on a par with the
more critical and dystopian images we will presently examine in the literary texts written by authors who lived and experienced Madrid's early
twentieth-century changes.

"Without a Style": Madrid's Modern Architectures

A building is a much more modest undertaking than the reorganization of an entire city and its surrounding regions. But it is notoriously
difficult to characterize the architecture of Madrid during the first third
of the twentieth century. Architectural historian Carlos de San Antonio believes there are three main tendencies in the architecture of

Madrid between 1914 and 1936: Rationalism, Regionalism and Classicism. He concludes his *Veinte años de arquitectura en Madrid. La edad de plata: 1918-1936,* however, with a chapter on what are now considered Madrid's most important architects of the period: Casto Fernández Shaw, Luis Guitiérrez Soto, Luis Martínez Feduchi and Vicente Eced. The title of the chapter "Personalidades al margen" [Marginal Personalities], is curious, because these architects built some of the most visually prominent and symbolically important parts of the Madrid skyline that still exist today.

These architects built buildings of vastly different styles. The more grandiose ultimately served to make names for the architects, and the more avant-garde, experimental, unique structures featured in *AC* were constructed for private individuals and were chances for the architects to put forth a more personal creative effort. Fernández Shaw, for example, picked up on avant-garde tendencies and added some regional, more personal touches. Unlike most other avant-garde architects of the time, he also paid attention to his surroundings. He railed against Le Corbusier's impersonal glass boxes for living in the 1928 special edition of *La Gaceta Literaria*, for example, saying emphatically: "¡¡¡Capitalistas!!! ¡¡¡He aquí la nueva arquitectura!!! ¡¡¡Buena, bonita, barata!!!... Nuestra carácter (español) individualista es enemigo de la casa en serie. Todos queremos los zapatos a medida y ... ¡claro!... vamos descalzos" [Capitalists!!! I have your new architecture here!!! Good, pretty, cheap!!! Our (Spanish) individualistic character is the enemy of the mass-produced house. Everyone wants their shoes to fit properly and ... of course! We will go barefoot] (3). His Gasolinera Porto Pi [Porto Pi Gas Station], constructed in 1927 on Alberto Aguilera Street in the Goya neighborhood of Madrid is considered one of the first (although perhaps not the most ambitious) instances of Modern architecture in Spain. According to Fernández Shaw himself,

> No tiene ningún estilo. Ha surgido una silueta de los elementos que integran la construcción. La superimposición de los planos de las marquesinas recuerda las alas de un biplano. La torre recuerda los tubos de ventilación de los barcos.... Unos faroles de línea sencilla animan las marquesinas; los aparatos que suministran la gasolina, el petróleo, los aceites,

el agua, el aire a presión, los extintores de incendio, decoran la instalación. Los automóviles, el altavoz, las luces le darán vida. (Urrutia 1997: 315)

> [It has no style. A silhouette has emerged from the elements that make up the construction. The superimposition of the planes of the different levels of the roof makes one think of the wings of a biplane. The tower reminds you of the central ventilation pipe of a ship.… The simple lines of the lights light up the levels of the roof; the equipment that delivers the gasoline, the oil, the water, the air under pressure, the fire extinguishers all decorate the facility. The automobiles, the loudspeaker, the lights give it life.]

This poetic description of Modern architecture's love affair with technology, which appears in the streamlined allusions to all that moves and looks stylishly futuristic, stands in stark contrast to his work with his mentor Antonio Palacios on the Círculo de Bellas Artes and the more staid Coliseum Building, located on the Gran Vía. Gutiérrez Soto's work is similar in that it is eclectic. He designed some of Madrid's most important structures devoted to leisure, including the Cine Barceló and the Piscina de la Isla, a massive swimming pool and beach development located on Madrid's Manzanares River. These Modernist structures were featured in avant-garde architectural journals such as *AC* but his bread and butter really came from the design of apartment buildings.

As can be seen, the contrast between these architects' more mainstream, big-money projects and their smaller, more avant-garde buildings is great. By designing gas stations and movie theaters, they were building places to service the symbols of capitalist accumulation *par excellence*. Once again, in an attempt to revolt against capital, capital is required, and the avant-garde style only becomes incorporated into this constant re-processing of the new and stylish in a constant commodification of artistic expression. Angel Urrutia emphasizes this when he repeats three times throughout his lengthy volume that

> los acontecimientos o regímenes políticos influyen menos de lo que parece en la auténtica arquitectura. Sería impropio e impreciso hablar en nuestro siglo tanto de *Arquitectura Alfonso XIII* como de *Arquitectura republicana*, *Arquitectura franquista* y menos de *Arquitectura Juan Carlos I*. (1997: 139)

[the historical events or the political regimes have much less of an influence than one might think on real architecture. It would be inappropriate and incorrect to talk about an *Architecture of Alfonse XIII*, a *Republican Architecture*, *Franquist Architecture*, or even more ridiculous to talk about an *Architecture of Juan Carlos I*.]

It is significant that the section of his often-quoted book on Madrid is called "Madrid: el estilo no hallado" [Madrid: Without a Style], where he mentions Nationalism, Modernism, Classicism, Imperialism and Art Deco as influential architectural styles that coexisted and can still be seen side by side on the Gran Vía. This further emphasizes the argument presented at the beginning of this chapter – that while the design of the urban environment needs to be thought of in its political context, it is capital and its circulation that ultimately shapes the culture of Madrid during the early twentieth century.

What exactly does the architecture of Madrid look like? With a trained eye, one can walk up the Gran Vía from the Plaza de Cibeles to the Plaza de España and feel as if one were walking through the evolution of Spanish architectural styles from the first third of the twentieth century. There were three sections, or big pushes, to the full extension of the 1,316 meters of the Gran Vía, begun in earnest in 1910 and not completed until 1954. Let us take a walk, then, up the Gran Vía's chaotic maze of competing styles in order to look at four iconic buildings: the Edificio "Metrópolis" (1905-1911), the "Edificio Telefónica" (1926-1930), the "Edificio Capitol," (1931-1933), and the "Edificio España" (1945-1947). This walk through space and time demonstrates how Madrid's architectural styles evolved from eclectic neo-baroque and French art nouveau-influenced Classicism to neo-imperialist Rationalism to Art Deco. According to Urrutia,

una vez la aristocracia y la alta burguesía deciden ocupar el Ensanche y se instalan en palacetes o en casas de viviendas, la Gran Vía trazada por el casco antiguo, entre la Calle de Alcalá y la actual Plaza de España, es ocupada en un evidente clima de especulación por edificios de viviendas que posteriormente van a ser forzados a transformarse en comercios y oficinas, pero sobretodo por edificios de recreo, hoteles, teatros y cines, los cuales van manifestando en sí mismos las misma paulatina evolución de la arquitectura venidera. (1997: 151)

[once the aristocracy and the upper middle class decide to occupy the extension of the Gran Vía and they move into mansions or residential housing, the Gran Vía coming off of the historic center between Alcalá Street and what is now the Plaza de España, is involved in investing in what had previously been housing that was transformed into recreational buildings, hotels, theaters and movie houses, which in turn exhibited the same architectural evolution.]

The Edificio Metrópolis, or Edificio de "La Unión y el Fenix," located on the Calle de Alcalá and the Calle Caballero de Gracia (of previously-mentioned *zarzuela* fame) was constructed between 1905 and 1911. Designed by the brothers Jules and Raymond Fevrier, its French influence is predominant since the plans for the building won an international competition in 1905 held by a private French company. Like the other buildings to be examined here, it is a monumental advertisement for private capital. The building's ornate, neo-baroque presence at the very beginning of one's ascent from the Plaza Cibeles, the single word "Metrópolis," seems a bold announcement for the Gran Vía in its entirety. Its cupola clearly identifies the building with the nineteenth century, as does the classical and neo-baroque ornamentation typical of the grand temples of business in Paris (Urrutia 1997: 133).

It is common in histories of Spanish architecture to mark the construction of the Edificio de la Telefónica as the beginning of Modern architecture in Spain. Designed by a Spaniard, Ignacio de Cárdenas Pastor, its construction was influenced by the use of materials newly proven in New York. International Telephone and Telegraph (ITT), an American company, purchased the newly-formed and capital-poor Compañía Telefónica Nacional de España in 1925. The American company wanted to construct a building in the very center of the busiest part of town in no small part so that the building itself could be an advertisement for the new corporation (Urrutia 1997: 153-155).

From the very beginning ITT insisted on running the Compañía Telefónica along American-style guidelines, and from the very beginning
they met with resistance. The contentious history of the façade of the
imposing building is a pivotal struggle over the shape of modern
Madrid. The project was initially given to both Cárdenas and his mentor at the Escuela de Madrid, Juan Moya Idigoras. The Spanish Compañía Telefónica wanted the building to have, as Urrutia puts it, "una
fachada monumental y representativa a la española, dentro del estilo
regionalista" [a monumental façade which was representative of Spain,
in the regional style] (1997: 154). This was Moya's specialty, a kind of
"organic" neo-baroque of the sort seen on the Metrópolis building.
The Americans at ITT rejected this idea, however, and because they
were the chief investors, dropped Moya from the project and sent the
younger Cárdenas to New York to study with ITT's renowned architect Louis S. Weeks. The result is what we see today: an American-
looking, functional stone monument to international capital. It was
constructed by Spanish workers but under the instruction of the
American building company Clark, MacMullen and Riley with amaz-
ing speed using the latest techniques in reinforced concrete (Urrutia
1997: 154).

The Carrión or Capitol building, constructed between 1931 and
1933, is perhaps the most emblematically Modern of all of the buildings on the Gran Vía. (*Fig. 2.4*) Built to house an impressive movie
house, it was also home to offices, cafeterias, cafes, private residences,
a hotel and a banquet hall. It is considered one of the best examples
of avant-garde Art Deco in all of Europe (Urrutia 1997: 329-331). Its
architects Luis Feduchi and Vicente Eced managed to add to the land-
scape of Madrid in a significant way. Major corporations – mostly international – have always paid top dollar to put their advertisements
on the façade of the Capitol Building. A study of the evolution of the
building's façade could read as a history of Spain's entrance into modern capitalism. Sixteen stories tall, it was constructed with the latest
American and German techniques and technology, using reinforced
concrete. Its exterior is of metal and stone: granite from Colmenar,
blue rock from Murcia, and Spanish marble. The importance of the
building to the development of urban consciousness in Madrid cannot

be overstated. The popular film magazine *Cinegramas* says of the building in 1934:

> Va a cumplirse el aniversario de la fecha en que fue inaugurado el Capitol. Aquel día significó ya un jalón en la historia del nuevo Madrid. Madrid, aquel día, dio un paso gigantesco en su camino de gran ciudad del mundo. Fue entonces cuando nuestra ciudad flirteó con Cosmópolis y cuando las luces de Nueva York se encendieron sobre la villa del piropo y del mantón. Sobre el mar abigarrado de la Gran Vía—multitud, escaparates, anuncios luminosos—avanzaba gallardamente, como un penacho de la vida suntuosa del mundo, la nave magnífica del nuevo edificio... Ese tramo de la Gran Vía que se ampara bajo la gran sombra internacional del Capitol, ¿no es una etapa nueva en la vida de la ciudad? Terrazas, escaparates, mujeres, han de reflejar, necesariamente en ese sitio, el estilo nuevo del gran edificio, como si éste proyectase sobre todo lo de su alrededor la influencia de su lujo. ("Un justo homenaje" 4)

> [The anniversary of the completion of the Capitol is approaching. That day was a landmark in the history of the new Madrid. That day, Madrid took a huge step on its path to becoming a great city of the world. It was then that our city flirted with Cosmopolis and then that the lights of New York lit up our humble town. On the many-colored sea of the Gran Vía – the crowd, the display windows, lighted advertisements – there gallantly advanced, like a proud and worldly being, the magnificent vessel of the new building.... That part of the Gran Vía that is protected by the shadow of the Capitol building, is it not a new stage in the life of the city? Patios, window displays, women, all must of necessity reflect the new style of the grand building, as if it projected on all of its surroundings a sense of its luxury.]

The cinematic look of the building[10] – the look of most Art Deco buildings–is aerodynamic, but in this case exaggeratedly so because

---

10. In one of many instances of Madrid's urban development and film industry being interdependent, the architect Feduchi also happened to be one of Spain's most important movie set designers, working on such films as Luis Marquina's 1936 *El bailarín y el trabajador,* Carlos Fernández Cuenca's *Leyenda rota* (1939) and José Luis Sáenz de Heredia's 1941 *Raza* (Cinemedia).

the building seems to rise higher and higher as the pedestrian walks up the Gran Vía from the Plaza Cibeles. This effect is accentuated when the tallest part of the sixteen-story building – the beacon – is brightly illuminated at night. Feduchi and Eced studied Art Deco design in France and Germany before their plan won the international competition held by the owner of the plot of land (Ignacio Carrión, Marquis of Melín). The lighting designer, Francisco Benito Delgado, a long-time collaborator of Feduchi, studied lighting and electric wiring in Amsterdam and Hamburg. He was central to another reason why the building was so popular: it was the first fully air-conditioned building in Madrid.

The Edificio España, designed by the brothers José María (the engineer) and Julián (the architect) Otamendi, was finished in 1947. The accompanying Torre de Madrid was finished in 1954. These enormous buildings mark the end of the Gran Vía. Urrutia calls them the ultimate "referencia a la prosperidad Nortemericana" [reference to North American prosperity] (439) because they were the tallest and widest of the cathedral-like stone skyscrapers built, like the Telefónica, with American-tested reinforced concrete and I-beams. The buildings face the Plaza de España, where there is a monument to Spain's literary cornerstone, Miguel de Cervantes. It is ironic that a tribute to an author so important to Spain is dwarfed by such American-looking monuments to foreign capital and military control (for these were the purposes that the buildings originally served). Furious debates followed the completion of these buildings as to whether they would stand the test of time. Architects in Spanish magazines of the early fifties had opposing views:

> Quiero defender el rascacielos porque me parece un logro de la técnica y está lleno de posibilidades y encantos. Sus errores no son de él, sino del mal uso que de él se hace. Creo que es una maravilla vivir en un piso cincuenta, sin polvo ni ruidos, sobre un valle con la ciudad abajo, a pocos segundos de un ascensor tanto como en una casa de campo junto a un bosque. (1956: Picardo 440)

> [I want to defend the skyscraper because it seems to me a technological achievement and it is full of possibilities and charm. Its mistakes are

not its fault, but that of the poor use to which it is put. I think that it is miraculous to live on the fiftieth floor, with neither noise nor dust, overlooking the valley of the city below, a few seconds away from an elevator just like in a country house next to the forest.]

On the other side of the argument, however, were statements such as the following by Miguel Fisac, an architect who wrote that "me opongo rotundamente al rascacielos porque es símbolo de una cultura y de una civilización que están podridas y llamadas a desaparecer" [I strenuously oppose the skyscraper because it is the symbol of a culture and a civilization that are rotten and can only fail] (44).

Madrid between 1900 and 1936 is built, designed and imagined, always conscious of its role as a center of power as the nation's capital and following a curious mix of traditional, monumental, classical and modern styles. These buildings, in their international modernity and in their Spanish uniqueness, make Madrid the city it is and are points of reference for the city's inhabitants, as we will see when they appear repeatedly in creative works about the modern experience. Behind the construction of space and place in Madrid lie certain visions for the future. What kind of culture, and what kind of values were staged on these streets, in these buildings? The texts examined here show how the values imbued in the culture of Madrid are often complex and sometimes contradictory, but always urban, modern and international, with either a hint of the transgressive or an obsession with the new that ties in perfectly with the increasingly industrial city and its newly-empowered and rapidly-growing middle class. A modern backdrop was built on the Gran Vía which in many ways was a set on which new relations of power were to play various roles, where ideologies would compete and new forms of culture would emerge. Simultaneously, whole sections of the city housing whole classes of people were left to their own devices, to develop chaotically into the problems of the future.

The three authors who will presently be discussed (Carmen de Burgos, José Díaz Fernández and Andrés Carranque de Ríos) are all of the opinion, much like in the *zarzuela* mentioned at the beginning of this chapter, that true progress and human emancipation in the name of modernity would come about in Spain "on the thirtieth of February, or when a frog grows hair." The period in question here was one of intense creativity and dynamism. It was also a period of marked economic hardship and economic inequality. It cannot be denied, however, that despite extenuating economic circumstances, a more modern Madrid was constructed, the old Madrid revamped, and various competing views from a range of class and gender positions of what it meant to be a modern, urban citizen were being represented in various forms of Spanish culture, both high and low.

Toward the end of the period under consideration, the seeds of political extremism were beginning to bear bitter fruit in Spain. One chilling example of this is Ernesto Giménez Caballero's 1935 treatise on art and architecture, *Arte y Estado*. During the 1920s and 1930s, Giménez Caballero was key to the formation of Madrid's experimental Cine-Club and the editor of the important journal *La Gaceta Literaria*. He eventually became one of the primary members of the Ministry of Culture during the first years of the Franco regime, but even before that happened, his ideological stance towards the avantgarde was telling. He proposed that Spanish art consisted primarily of painting and sculpture, ignoring new technologies such as photography and film. He said the avant-garde was in a state of decline, although he put great stock in the architecture of Le Corbusier.[11] In *Arte y Estado* he fearfully argues that the so-called New Architecture of Gropius and Mies van de Rohe was created by "el espíritu judío y socialista y la enseñanza de 1917" [the Jewish and Socialist spirit of the teachings of 1917] (1935: 95) but he believes that salvation rested in the sisterhood of Italy and Spain, with their Catholic genius, where a tradition of functionality would lead to a stark, massive and proportional architecture. In this he was right: a hybrid Imperial, Italian-influenced architectural style would eventually come to extol the supposed glory of Francoist Spain. Culture would be used as a symbol of political power and dominance in the 1940s. Some artists and

---

11. See Santiáñez for a close literary analysis of the architectural terms used in the Fascist writing of Giménez Caballero.

intellectuals were forced to leave the country after the Spanish Civil War of 1936-39. Some died in the fight. Some managed to find places for themselves within the new rhetoric of the 1940s and 1950s. Whatever the case, with the cultural continuity so abruptly broken by the war, it would take another generation to pick up the pieces and Madrid would take on a very different look and feel.

CHAPTER III

Entering Modernity with Carmen de Burgos

Carmen de Burgos Seguí was one of Spain's most widely known cultural figures of her day, despite her almost complete omission from Spanish literary history.[1] She was a prolific writer, producing twelve novels, over one hundred popular novellas and stories, and a variety of essays on politics, social values, cooking, letter writing, etiquette, travel, and women's issues. She earned a reputation as a polemical author during the early decades of the twentieth century. Her life is indicative of the ways in which the rapid social and political changes of a modernizing Spain shifted the parameters for potential women writers, with respect not only to the kinds of literature they might write, but also to the practice of writing as a profession.

Burgos's fictional representation of Madrid is unique. Her experience of Madrid—its community of artists as well as the details of the everyday lives of men, women and children—was different than that

---

1. Ugarte deals with some of the reasons there are so few women writers present in the traditional canon at the turn of the century ("The Generational Fallacy"). For authoritative discussions of nineteenth- and early twentieth-century gender and canonicity see Bieder and Pérez (1993).

of her male contemporaries and since there are relatively few women who wrote so proficiently and prolifically about Madrid at the turn of the century, her work warrants close attention. The three texts chosen for analysis in this chapter are very different from one another. *La rampa* (1917), one of her twelve full-length novels, focuses on the lives of working women and how they are forced to adapt (sometimes successfully, but more often unsuccessfully) to the changing social values and economic realities of Madrid in the '10s and '20s. *Los negociantes de la Puerta del Sol* (1919) focuses on the construction of place as outlined in Chapter One of this study and the way it forms human consciousness in an increasingly industrial and urban society, while *El veneno del arte* (1910), an autobiographical work, is primarily a critique of the creative, intellectual class of the capital and how the increased reproducibility of art in the city begins to change the very nature of art itself.

The 'Nueva Mujer Moderna' Enters the Public Sphere

The increasing pace of modernization of Spanish society in the early twentieth century entailed significant modifications in economic, social and demographic structures. This brought about changes in social structures and the transformation of cultural modes and values which, in turn, generated modifications in the ideological discourse on women. The traditional representation of woman as the "Ángel del Hogar" [Angel of the Hearth] was challenged by a new gender discourse based on what was called the "Nueva Mujer Moderna" [New Modern Woman], an "ideal" woman already in vogue in many European countries and in North America (Nash 1999: 25-50). This notion of the modern woman was prevalent in many publications of the time and was defended enthusiastically by women such as Burgos in her *La mujer moderna y sus derechos* (1927).

Although not as widely accepted as the traditional "Ángel del Hogar," this new cultural representation was incorporated into social values and collective imagery about gender norms. The redefinition of women in terms of modernity was an effective way of talking about women within the new social, political, economic and demographic concerns of the city. The shift from the old model of femininity to the innovative "Nueva Mujer Moderna" allowed women to adjust to the process of modernity. It accommodated restrictive gender roles toward the new needs of the labor market and society. This readjustment was a functional mechanism which allowed women access to specific areas of public activity such as education, culture and new sectors of the labor market. It thus responded to the new socioeconomic needs of Spanish society and, in this way, became part of hegemonic discourse on women. Despite its modernizing effect, however, Nash stresses that the model of the "Nueva Mujer Moderna" also maintained the core of traditional gender identity by defining women as primarily and essentially mothers and childbearers, albeit in a new way (1983: 37).

The vast majority of women between 1900 and 1930 in Spain did not hold regular, full-time employment outside of the home. Historians note that Spain's formal workforce was more heavily masculine than that of other Western European countries.[2] Female employment outside of the home contradicted all of the precepts of ideal womanhood and threatened to topple one of the pillars of masculine legitimacy. Geraldine Scanlon, in her meticulous study of women in Spain *Polémica feminista en España* says that at the turn of the century

> la idea muy difundida de que el trabajo de la mujer era degradante (creencia que estaba muy arraigada entre la clase media) suponía una formidable barrera psicológica.... La deshonra de tener que trabajar era aún mayor si la mujer estaba casada, pues no sólo se humillaba ella, sino también su marido. (1976: 9)

> [the widely disseminated idea that women's work was degrading (a belief that was strong among the middle class) involves a formidable psycho-

---

2. Capel Martínez presents concrete data about working women in Madrid during this period. She estimates that in 1900 14.8% of all women in the capital are working outside of the home, while in 1930 the number decreases to 13.2% (216).

logical barrier…. The dishonor of having to work was even greater if the
woman was married, since it was not only a humiliation for her, but for
her husband as well.]

As is made clear in the work of Burgos analyzed here, a double standard distinguished between what was acceptable for middle and
upper class women versus women of a less economically privileged
class.

For the middle and upper classes at the turn of the century, chari-
table volunteerism, much of it organized through the Church, was
the only acceptable work for a "respectable" woman. Few women
were breaking barriers to enter the professions. The first professions
to open their doors to more than a handful of women were the least
prestigious such as nursing and midwifery, pharmacy and elementary
school teaching. These jobs were almost exclusively reserved for
unmarried women. Women doctors were gradually accepted into certain fields such as gynecology and pediatrics, where it was argued that
they could better preserve the chastity of female patients, but their
numbers were significantly lower than in other countries in Europe
and in the United States. Fewer women took up law—in fact, by the
time of the Second Republic, only two women had ever appeared in
court, according to Nash (1999: 36-40). More than in the professions, middle-class women began to find increasing employment in
lower-paid areas of the expanding service economy, in either the public or private sector. In 1882 the state decreed that women could be
hired to work in telegraph and postal service areas. Not until 1917
could they compete for civil service positions, however, and then only
as assistants.

Many more women from poor families entered the workforce at
some point during their lifetime, usually before marriage. Like most
European countries at the turn of the century, the two sectors that
employed the most women were domestic service and agriculture. It is
worth noting that in Spain there was not a sharp female transfer from
these sectors to more industrial and public service jobs later in the
first third of the century. While the number of female agriculture
workers did drop dramatically, these women did not appear in other

categories. Additionally, although there are no labor statistics for women for the Republican period, this decline probably continued through the Depression into the 1930s.[3]

In Madrid, the fate of the women who tried to support themselves as shop clerks or office workers was grim. There was an essential contradiction in these women—usually young—who thought of themselves as somewhat progressive, doing jobs that before had been done by men, many of them living independently and having the freedom to make important choices about their lives. Margarita Nelken points out in *La condición social de la mujer en España*, however, that there is another side to this experience.

> Esta clase de empleadas, naturalmente la más numerosa, tiene en Madrid unos sueldos que rechazaría con indignación cualquier 'treintarrealera' que viene a servir y llega del pueblo, pues ésta, por escaso que sea el sueldo, recibe además alojamiento y manutención. Empleadas españolas: mecanógrafas, tenedoras de libros, cajeras, dependientas, todas vosotras, tan humildes en vuestro pobre traje de señoritas, venidas a menos, tan anémicas y tan fieles y tan valientes, tan íntegras, sin siquiera el consuelo de los alegres noviazgos modisteriles, demasiado altas y demasiado empequeñecidas, sois la más pura y la más desconsoladora representación de la condición social de la mujer en España. (1922: 38-39)

> This kind of female employee, usually in the majority, receives salaries that any 'thirty-something' maid who came to work from the countryside would reject with indignation because they, although they receive a low wage, get lodging and food on top of that. Spanish female employees: typists, bookkeepers, cashiers, clerks, all of you, so humble in your shabby clothes, who are down on your luck, so anemic and so faithful and so brave, so whole, without even the solace of a stylish and happy

---

3. Nash (1983) argues that this demonstrates a strong cultural resistance to women workers, even under the Leftist Civil War administrations, when women were rarely trained to replace men in skilled industrial jobs when the latter went to the front, as happened in the United States. Despite complaints by activist women's organizations like *Mujeres Antifascistas,* it appears that few women crossed over into male jobs, even under the special demands of the wartime economy.

courtship, too tall and too small, you are the purest and the most incon-
solable representation of the social condition of the Spanish woman.]

In a society that assumed that all women were either married or prepar-
ing to be married, it was commonly thought that jobs held by women
were only temporary. For this reason, women employees were not val-
ued highly and were poorly compensated. Prostitution was a constant
temptation for many unskilled young women who did not feel they
could support themselves through work in an office or store.[4]

In Cristóbal's study "Las mujeres en el comercio madrileño del
primer tercio del siglo XX" (1986: 225-248), she examines how
increasing numbers of women between 1900 and 1930 began to
work in Madrid. Widows made up the largest percentage of this
group. The second group most likely to work were those ages 18-30,
while the women least likely to work were those who were married. It
is important to note that Cristóbal credits ambitious business owners
more than feminist groups and changing ideas about women in Spanish society with this increase in women's employment in the business
sectors.

A lo largo del primer tercio del siglo XX, se produce un crecimiento
del número de mujeres empleadas en establecimientos mercantiles, con
salarios muy inferiores a los de la dependencia masculina. Este hecho no
es exclusivo del mundo del comercio, sino una característica común del
trabajo femenino de la época. Se puede decir que el deseo patronal de
contar con mano de obra barata encontró el terreno abandonado para
ello en la situación social de las mujeres. (1986: 323)

[Through the first third of the twentieth century, the number of
women employed in sales establishments grew, but with salaries much

---

4. Capel Martínez (1986) outlines the reasons many young women became prosti-
    tutes in major Spanish cities between 1900 and 1930. While she and other histo-
    rians are of the opinion that prostitution was one of the most significant ways
    women made money for themselves outside of the home, they also agree that it
    has proven difficult for historians to document this with accuracy.

lower than the male employees. This doesn't just happen in the commercial professions, but it is a common factor of women's work of the time period. You could say that the employer's desire for cheap labor found fertile ground in the changing social situation of women.]

It is important to remember that social values do not change in a vacuum, as Cristóbal's work shows. Rather, changing ideas about women were closely tied to capital and new ways of exchanging goods and services in the urban context.

Madrid 1900 – 1930: The Other Side of the City

The everyday lives of all of Madrid's citizens between 1900 and 1930 were much like those of the inhabitants of the large cities of other rapidly-industrializing countries. The lives of the poor and lower-middle class were astoundingly difficult. It is against the ills of the city at the turn of the century that the discipline of modern urban planning was born, as discussed in Chapter Two. The problem was the injustice inherent in the economic inequality of the city itself. The perception of the city was that it was the source of multiple social evils, possible biological decline and potential political insurrection. Hall makes the point that

> poverty had been endemic since the beginning of society, but in the countryside it could be more or less hidden; once concentrated in the city, it was revealed.... In this sense industrialization and urbanization, as the Marxists always say, did create a new set of social relationships and a new set of social perceptions. (1988: 44-45)

Folguera Crespo describes a typical family home in Madrid during this period in her study "Revolución y Restauración. La emergencia de los primeros ideales emancipadores (1868-1931)":

> Son lugares en los que apenas se realizan caminos o transformaciones de generación en generación, y no existen espacios propios para cada uno de los miembros de la familia. Las condiciones de salubridad en este

tipo de viviendas son lamentables. A la ausencia de luz, de agua corriente y de alcantarillas debe añadirse además, la basura y los excrementos acumulados en las calles. Las mujeres de las clases populares, a diferencia de las mujeres de la burguesía, no pueden disfrutar de la intimidad, de la privacidad del hogar. Los espacios privados, los espacios femeninos se encuentran a caballo entre el propio hogar y el patio, la corrala o la calle: lo que permite a las mujeres que habitan estos barrios desarrollar fácilmente lazos de solidaridad y de sociabilidad. Gran parte de las tareas domésticas tienen lugar en la calle: el lavado, el remendado de la ropa, la compra ..., sirviendo de pretexto para establecer relaciones de amistad y desarrollar, en su caso, redes solidarias entre personas de su entorno. (1997: 458)

[They are places where one hardly sees any progress or transformation from one generation to the other, and there are no differentiated spaces for family members. The health conditions in this type of housing are lamentable. To the absence of light, running water and sewers one can add the garbage and accumulation of excrement in the streets. The working class women, unlike the women of the middle class, cannot enjoy any intimacy or privacy in the home. Private spaces, femenine spaces can be found between the home and the patio, the *corrala* and the street: the places that allow the women who inhabit these neighborhoods to easily develop bonds of solidarity and sociability. A great number of domestic chores take place in the street; the washing, the mending of clothes, shopping ...; serving as a pretext for establishing friendships and forming close relationships with those around them.]

Contrast this description of the living and working spaces of the vast majority of women in Madrid with those of upper-class women, whom Folguera Crespo also describes:

Todas estas construcciones se realizan con criterios de racionalidad bien definidos. Materializan todas ellas las aspiraciones de un grupo social minoritario que desea con sus viviendas de carácter singular reflejar su situación privilegiada en la estructura social. Su construcción parte del concepto de diferenciación y funcionalización de los espacios en la búsqueda de la privacidad y el 'confort' hasta entonces desconocidos. Las fachadas presentan gran diversidad de ornamentación.... Pero quizás lo más innovador de este tipo de construcciones son los huecos de ventana que dan luminosidad, hasta entonces prácticamente inexistente en las construcciones urbanas. Estas viviendas constan de numerosas habitaciones: recibidor, despacho, biblioteca, salones, gabinetes y comedor, varias habitaciones destinadas a dormitorios. Las dependencias destinadas a servicio incluían cocina, despensa, baño y excusado. (1997: 459)

[All of these buildings were created with well-defined rational criteria. All of them put into material form the aspirations of a social minority that wants with their singular housing to reflect their own priviledged social structure. Their buildings stem from the concept of differentiation and funcionality of spaces in the creation of new notions of privacy and 'comfort'. The facades contain different types of ornamentation .... But perhaps the most innovative thing about these buildings is the window frames which provide light, something that was practically nonexistent in urban construction. These housing units had numerous rooms: an entrance, office, library, living rooms and a dining room, as well as various bedrooms. Houses with servants included a kitchen, pantry, bath and half-bath.]

The everyday living spaces of upper- and middle-class women were dramatically different from those of working-class women. Those women living with less were housed in extraordinarily multifunctional spaces with no privacy, in constant contact with their neighbors and spent much of their time in the street. Women belonging to families who had money lived in homes where there were strictly differentiated spaces for specific uses, they enjoyed a higher level of privacy and were far more sheltered from the city and one other. Burgos's fiction chronicles and critiques what these urban class- and gender-differentiated spaces meant for Madrid's citizens during this time period.

'La Nueva Literatura' and Mass Culture in Modern Madrid

Against this backdrop of the struggle for a healthy and meaningful way of life in the city, the modernization process of this period had inaugurated a boom in Spanish literature and remapped the relationship between the writer and the reading public. With increasing literacy a potential readership expanded across class and gender lines.[5] The growing middle class demanded cheap entertainment, provided by a proliferation of magazines dependent on advertising revenues, and popular prose collections were set up as commercial ventures. Novels for mass circulation were short and disposable. Production increased and many authors—including a handful of women— became professionals able to make a decent living from their writing. Their work reached the masses as never before and helped define what it was to live and work in Madrid.

Urioste describes middle-class Spanish readers as "una burguesía liberal que lee lo mismo una novela publicada, por ejemplo, en la colección *El Cuento Semanal* que asiste a una de las representaciones del teatro burgués de Jacinto Benavente" [the same liberal middle class that reads a novel, for example, published in *The Weekly Story* collection and then attends one of the bourgeois theatrical works by Jacinto Benavente] (1997: 27). The novel produced for middle-class consumption, she goes on to say, has three main characteristics:

> —en primer lugar, no podía ser muy larga, pues el público no dispone de mucho tiempo para la lectura—estamos en la época de la velocidad;
> —en segundo lugar, el producto novela debía venir envuelto en una hermosa cobertura, ya que el público lector le gustaba lo artístico. De la unión entre la literatura y el elemento artístico nació la portada de la novela: caricatura del autor o dibujo alusivo al tema de la novela. La edi-

---

5. Rates of illiteracy in Spain at the turn of the century were high compared to those of the rest of Europe, although they went down significantly between 1900 and 1930. An estimated 71.4 % of women and 55.8% of men were illiterate in 1900, while in 1930 47.5% of Spanish women and 37% of men were illiterate (Carr 1983: 289). These numbers reflect all regions of Spain, however. Illiteracy in Spain was much higher in rural than in urban areas. According to Fusi and Palafox there are no known reliable literacy statistics for Madrid between 1900 and 1936 (1997: 189).

torial complacía, así, al lector burgués que pensaba en la propiedad priva-
da de una pequeña obra de arte;

–por último, desde el punto de vista de las editoriales que
abastecían al público lector, era necesario crear el hábito de lectura y de
aquí la necesidad de adquirir la novela o viceversa. Para la consecución
de estos fines, se editaron colecciones de tirada semanal y de bajo costo.
(1997: 27)

[– in the first place, it couldn't be too long, because the public did
not have much time for reading – this is the age of speed;

– in the second place, the new product should be graced by a handsome cover because the reading public liked things that were artistic.
From the union of art and literature came the book cover: a caricature of
the author or a drawing that alluded to the theme of the novel. The press
made the middle-class reader happy this way, because they made a work
of art out of private property;

– lastly, from the point of view of the presses who supplied books to
their readers, it was necessary to feed their reading habit and the need to
acquire more reading material. To these ends, they edited weekly low-
cost series.]

Between 1900 and 1930 approximately 71 short novel collections of
this type were created. The most successful had names like *Biblioteca
patria de obras premiadas* (1904-30); *Los Contemporáneos* (1909-26);
El Cuento Semanal (1907-12): *El libro popular* (1912-16): *La novela
corta* (1916-25); *La novela de hoy* (1922-32); *La novela de la noche* (
1924-24); *La novela mundial* (1926-28); *La novela semanal* (1921-
25); and *Los novelistas* (1928-29) (Urioste 1997: 28). Urioste points
out that the "novela de entregas" [serialized novel] evolves into the
short novel because "era necesario buscar un sustituto para las entregas teniendo en cuenta el factor de un público lector urbano en su
mayoría mujeres" [it was necessary to look for a substitute for the
serialized novel that took into account the fact that most readers
were women who lived in the city] (28). Burgos owed her success as
a writer of fiction to these short novel series and to middle- and
upper-middle class women with disposable incomes and leisure
time. The modern city, as demonstrated in Chapters One and Two,

has a way of constantly creating and rendering obsolete forms of cultural production and expression. These short novel series too would be out of date by the 1940s and give way to other ways of marketing print culture.[6]

One is hard pressed to find any reference to Burgos in traditional literary histories of Spain written before 2000. De Nora's *La novela española contemporánea (1927-1939)*, calls her a "vulgarizadora ... de todo aquel feminismo, cientifismo, reformismo, etc., tan noble pero tan vagamente progresista" [vulgar influence ... with all of that feminism, scientific discourse, reform, etc., so noble but so vaguely liberal] (1979: 52-53). The reasons behind her absence are obvious. The ideology under which those in control of cultural dissemination functioned assured the selection of texts for the canon that bolstered their position in society.[7] The culture that those with the institutional power to form a canon sought to put the spotlight on works with largely Castilian-nationalist and Christian values. In addition, the concept of the literary generation adhered to by literary theorists such as Julius Petersen and Wilhelm Dilthey appeared in many pedagogical literary histories and is still used today as a way of organizing the aesthetic ebbs and flows of the last two hundred years of Spanish literature. The literary canon of the Franco period, in short, still influences the

---

6. For a history of the way literature was written and mass produced in the nineteenth century in the form of the serialized novel see Ferreras. Urioste describes the creation of new short novel series of the first decades of the twentieth century and goes into detail about three Andalusian authors who lived and worked in Madrid—Rafael Cansinos Assens, Carmen de Burgos and José Más—arguing that they belong to a new, expanded, more inclusive Spanish literary canon. Fernández Cifuentes writes about the marketing of literature during this period but does not comment on the most widely-read works, focusing instead on the small-scale diffusion of more intellectual, avant-garde or philosophical novels.

7. Blanco Aguinaga states that after 1939, ninety percent of all Spanish intellectuals were in exile, "entre ellos 110 profesores universitarios, 200 de instituto y 2.000 maestros" [among them 110 university professors, 200 high school teachers and 2,000 primary school teachers] (1979: 122). Some important novelists of the time who were forced to leave were Max Aub, Arturo Barea, Ramón Sender, Francisco Ayala, Benjamín Jarnés and Miguel Andújar, just to name a few.

way Spanish literature is taught today. Burgos, as has been argued, belongs to both the Generation of '98 and the avant-garde Generation of '27, yet at the same time belongs to neither (Ugarte, Bieder, Johnson). Her literature and essays voice anti-clerical sentiments and critique set notions about the roles of women and men in society. These works were completely ignored during the dictatorship and are still largely unknown today because it is oftentimes difficult to obtain texts by Burgos since there have been few new editions published and the existing original editions are in such poor condition that they are difficult to read.[8]

Carmen de Burgos was born in 1867[9] into a landowning family in eastern Andalusia (Almería). By her date of birth she could be considered a member of the Generation of '98, although her biographer Núñez Rey is of the opinion that "por su modernidad, compartía el pensamiento noventayochista sobrepasándolo – fue más que una escritora; fue un impulso histórico" [in terms of her modernity, she shared the thought of the Generation of '98 but she surpassed it – she was more than an author; she was an historic force] (37). Since her teenage years it was clear that Burgos had strong personal and professional ambitions. When she was sixteen she married Arturo Álvarez Bustos (a journalist twelve years her senior) against the wishes of her family. Despite her family obligations, she began to work as a typesetter at the press of a satirical newspaper called *Almería Bufa*, which belonged to her father-in-law. It was here that she first learned how to edit a newspaper and where she first became a journalist. In 1895 Burgos earned her degrees in primary and secondary education, and three years later she was granted a permanent position at the

---

8.   Almost all scholarship about Carmen de Burgos bemoans the fact that she is a forgotten literary figure. This is changing, however, with new editions of her writing and studies of her life appearing in print in recent years. See Bieder, Establier Pérez, Hardcastle, Johnson (2003), Larson (2006), Louis, Mangini (2001), Núñez Rey (2005), Rodríguez (1998) and Ugarte (1996).

9.   Burgos herself placed her birth date later and later as she grew older. Sources for biographical information include Castañeda, Establier Pérez and Núñez Rey.

Teacher's School in Guadalajara. During this period she began to write stories and essays, which she published in 1900 as a collection entitled *Ensayos literarios*. In this collection she included the essay "La educación de la mujer," [Women's Education] which prefigured the many later essays she would write on this same topic. Burgos, emboldened by her economic independence, left the abusive relationship she shared with her husband. With her young daughter, she left Almería for Guadalajara to start her double career as a teacher and author.

Her real objective, however, was to live and work in Madrid. She was able to do this in 1906, when she was granted a teaching position in the Teacher's School in the capital. After a time in Toledo, she would finally move to Madrid to occupy the position she would have for the rest of her life. Much of Burgos's feminist writing is based on the assumption that access to employment is the primary factor that enables women to achieve economic independence, and the author's writing and political activity can be seen as an attempt to make these conditions possible.[10]

Burgos was a prolific and tireless writer who accepted work as a translator, who engaged in investigative journalism, who wrote women's conduct manuals – anything she could get her hands on to support herself and her daughter. Her politics were tentatively liberal at the beginning of her writing career but became progressively more radical towards the end of her life. She participated actively in national politics and *tertulias* as early as 1902, when she became the first female journalist for the newspaper *Diario Universal*. Her first column was called "Lecturas para la mujer" [Women's Reading], where she talked about topics from the latest hairstyles and hats to the working

---

10. Folguera Crespo points out that for all of the advances in women's education stemming from new attitudes towards women espoused by the Instituto Libre de Enseñanza and Krausism, from 1900 to 1920 in Madrid, the average time a young girl spent in school was six months. This was mainly due, she explains, to the fact that girls were often needed in the home to take care of the family or to make money outside of the home to help in its upkeep (1997: 478).

conditions of the women making said finery. It is during this period that Augusto Figueroa, the editor of the newspaper, gave her the nickname "Colombine." In 1906 she began to write for another of the capital's important newspapers, *ABC*, and shortly thereafter she began two more important projects: her column "Femeninas" [Women's World] for *El Heraldo de Madrid*, the most widely-read of Madrid's serial publications, and her famous *tertulia*, "Los Miércoles de Colombine" [Colombine's Wednesdays]. Burgos does not begin to devote herself in any serious way to literature until 1907, when she publishes her first novel with the series *El Cuento Semanal* called *El tesoro del Castillo* [The Castle's Treasure]. Burgos owed her initial literary success to the many invitations of publisher Eduardo Zamacois to publish her work in such series as *La Novela Corta*, *La Novela Femenina* and *Los Contemporáneos*, all of which served the growing desire of the urban middle class for weekly reading material. In 1907 Burgos took the funds from her publications with Zamacois and founded her own magazine, *Revista Crítica*, and she began her long collaboration with Ramón Gómez de la Serna and his publication, *Prometeo*, which he began that same year. Two years later, Burgos would embark on a new adventure as a war correspondent in Morocco.

In order to achieve her professional goals, Burgos had to break many of the rules that were in place for Spanish women. She pushed, for example, for the right for women to divorce their husbands. She earned the nickname "La Divorciadora" [The Divorcer] after she conducted her famous survey on divorce in *El Heraldo de Madrid*. This nickname was replaced with another, "La Dama Roja" [The Red Lady] shortly thereafter, when she began publishing articles on the brutal conditions faced by migrants coming to the country's capital from the countryside. Burgos traveled often, oftentimes alone, to learn about other cultures but also to escape from the stress and exhaustion of the city. Her personal life also reflected this independence. She enjoyed a twenty-year personal and professional relationship with Gómez de la Serna, and for this she was the object of many cruel jokes since they never married and she was twenty years his senior. For many decades Burgos's enormously important writing was forgotten and she was usually referred to as simply the companion to the now better-known and undoubtedly canonical Gómez de la Serna. This is particularly ironic, taking into account what we know now about how Burgos first introduced Gómez de la Serna into Madrid's café society and how she would consistently and thoroughly edit his work for decades. Her personal life would become public in 1929 in an unwelcome way when the scandal broke that Gómez de la Serna had had an affair with Burgos's daughter while they were both working on his play *Los medios seres*.

After this personal and professional relationship of more than twenty years came to an end, Burgos began the most active and radical stage of her life. Her ideas about the right of women to vote changed over the course of her lifetime. Instead of maintaining her previous position (a common one in Spain at the time) that women should not be given the vote because they lack the education to know how to vote independently of their priests and husbands, Burgos became an ardent suffragist. She was elected the President of the Cruzada de Mujeres Españolas [Crusade for Spanish Women] and worked tirelessly for the Liga Internacional de Mujeres Ibéricas e Iberoamericanas [International League of Iberian and Iberoamerican Women] and she joined the Partido Republicano Radical Socialista [Radical Republican Socialist Party] in 1930. Within this party she continued to work for women's suffrage, the right to divorce, and continued to write against the death penalty. A popular story is that Burgos died shouting the words "¡Viva la República!" [Long Live the Republic!] defending her position at a political gathering in 1932. Whether or not this is the case, it is undeniable that Carmen de Burgos, through her life and work, pushed constantly at the boundaries of what the modern woman was allowed to do.

Negotiating the Street in *La rampa*

The dedication with which *La rampa* begins reads: "A toda esa multitud de mujeres desvalidas y desorientadas, que han venido a mí, preguntándome qué camino podrían tomar, y me han hecho sentir su tragedia" [To all the multitude of needy and lost women who have come to me asking which path they should take, and have introduced me to their tragedies]. It is a *bildunsgroman* of the women who came to Madrid to work at newly-opened positions as office clerks, sales-girls and maids at the beginning of the century. *La rampa* is about two women, Isabel and Águeda, who live together in difficult circumstances and work on the Calle del Carmen in a "Bazar," the name for a type of early department store. They work and spend what little free time they have on the Calle del Carmen and the Calle Preciados, two parallel streets immediately off of the Puerta del Sol where, between approximately 1890 and 1920, the commercial center of the city was located. While it is true that there was an economic boom in Spain during World War One due to the country's neutrality, inflation was high and wages low. The novel offers a detailed list of expenses for the working women of this period that provides great insight into their way of life.

Alquiler del modesto cuarto . . . . 25,00 ptas.
Luz 2,0
Una arroba de carbón al mes para calentar
el agua y lavarse 2,70
Medio abono, para comer las mañanas,
en el rest. Babilonia 30,00
Propina para los camareros 2,00
Ropa limpia 2,50
Café para desayuno 2,25
Leche condensada 1,50
Azúcar 1,40
Pan, todo el mes, para el desayuno
y la comida de la tarde 4,50
Alcohol de quemar 2,00
Sesenta céntimos diarios para la cena, hacían al mes 18,00

Rent for modest room . . . . 25.00 ptas.
Light 2.00
Twenty-five pounds of coal for heating
water and washing 2.70
Partial meal ticket, to eat every morning,

in the Babilonia Rest 30.00
Tips for waiters 2.0
Laundry 2.50
Breakfast coffee 2.25
Condensed milk 1.50
Sugar 1.40
Bread for the month, for breakfast and lunch 4.50
Burning alcohol 2.00
(1917: 27)

Águeda is the orphaned daughter of working-class parents who migrated from the countryside while Isabel's working class status is a new experience for her, but both women face the challenges of living in a city where they have no choice but to be independent.

Michael Ugarte points out the differences between *La rampa* and other socially critical urban novels of the time not only in terms of the narrative's construction but how Madrid is represented.

> The narrator makes no pretense of sociological objectivity or scientific indifference as tends to be the case in Baroja's series of Madrid novels *La lucha por la vida*. The story is not an objective one, and the reader does not expect it to be so. Yet at the same time, in keeping with urban writing, the author receives a tangible sociological reality that she wants her readers to acknowledge regardless of gender. (1994: 271)

Almost all of *La rampa* consists of stories told by female narrators about their lives in the city. The problems that they try to solve are those of any inhabitant of the modern city, however. The title of the first chapter, "El comedor de todos," illustrates this broader, more collective perspective, for example.

Madrid is hostile to the primary and secondary characters of *La rampa*. Looking for new ways to live in the city, every single one of them feels as if they are charting new ground. Young and single, they are vulnerable and seen as immoral because they lack the protection of a male family member. At one point in the novel, Isabel has no choice but to admit herself to a hospital for unwed mothers on the Calle de Embajadores, in the neighborhood of Lavapiés. She is pregnant with the child of a young professional who has abandoned her. This four-chapter segment of the novel goes into great detail about how the city has both a psychological and physical impact on women.

Whether walking down the street or eating in a restaurant, Isabel and Águeda are the targets of sexual harassment. The constant threat of gender-based violence on the street and other public spaces exhausts them. At one point in the novel, Isabel is arrested for no other reason than that she is a woman on the street at night on the Calle Huertas and the police therefore assume that she is a prostitute.[11] Mistaken for a prostitute, Isabel is forced to suffer yet another humiliation as she is carted off to jail along with other women who find themselves in the same situation. The fact that the police sweep up a crowd of women unites them all and emphasizes that no woman, regardless of class, is safe on the city streets.

The overall tone of the novel is didactic and somber. There are, however, more hopeful moments when the women see that the city does offer its small freedoms. Águeda goes through many of the same trials as her best friend Isabel, but in spite of this she is able to survive through the support of her friend and her relationship (significantly outside of marriage) with a young intellectual revolutionary. Isabel is not so fortunate. The challenge of trying to raise a child on her own proves to be too much for her. She has no recourse but to become a hired mother for another family – a governess. In the powerful final scene she is fired for scolding the children under her care because they have made fun of a drunk woman in front of their home. Her last option, one that is presented as one even worse than prostitution, is to admit herself to the city's poorhouse for women, where maids are trained and then hired into service for the middle class.

There is a very strong sense of place in *La rampa (Fig. 3.1)*. Isabel and Águeda make their meager living as shop girls in a small depart-

---

11. A double standard that simultaneously imposed a process of medical registration and encouraged the vigilance and prosecution of prostitutes in Spain went largely unquestioned, as Capel Martínez points out in her study "Mujer y trabajo en la España de Alfonso XIII" (1986: 265-298).

ment store but when they have the chance to rest for a few minutes, they go window shopping and dream of what they would do with the very goods they sell but cannot afford.

> Empezaron a andar, siguiendo la Calle del Carmen, en dirección a la Puerta del Sol, y bien pronto olvidaron su disgusto para distraerse con la contemplación de los transeúntes y de los escaparates, con fuerza de expansión juvenil, acortando el paso, como si disfrutara un paseo y quisiera retardar el momento de llegar al Bazar, donde habían de quedar sepultadas todo el resto del día. (1917: 20)

> [They began to walk, following the Calle del Carmen, towards the Puerta del Sol, and soon they forgot their annoyance and distracted themselves by watching the passersby and the display windows and like kids having fun, with shorter steps, as if they were enjoying a walk and wanted to slow down time before they got to the Bazar, where they had to remain buried for the rest of the day.]

When this novel was written, the Puerta del Sol was the center of commerce and café culture in Madrid, and had been for some time. The feeling that this was about to change, however, was in the air. In a chapter called "El cochero cínico" [The Cynical Coach Driver], Fernando and Isabel take a tour of the city on a day off, during the Verbena del Carmen. This is a relatively disjointed chapter during which the words of the driver are interspersed with Isabel's first-person narration where she reveals that she is half-heartedly trying to avoid the insistent, roving hands of Fernando. Because the two main characters are not speaking, the reader listens to what the driver has to say about the most important restructuring going in Madrid: namely, the development of the Gran Vía and the prolongation of the Castellana.

> Habían entrado por las calles nuevas el ensanche que se abren hacia la Guindalera y Alcalá. El cochero cínico, en su papel de diablo cojuelo, iba contándoles historias de gentes que vivían en aquellas casas. –Esto va a ser la alegría de Madrid—decía-. A todas las palomitas que vivían por el centro las han echado de allí y se han venido aquí, donde viven mejor.

Les iba dando detalles de las casas, de los merenderos de alto coturno, donde se divertía la aristocracia. Los albergues más burgueses, con comida y habitaciones amuebladas, que no inquietaba la policía; y los merenderos económicos, paraíso de criaditas treintarrealeras y de soldados pobres, que no podían aspirar a más. (1917: 109)

[They started down the new streets that open up towards Guindalera and Alcalá. The cynical driver, in his role as a kind of gossiping troublemaker, started telling stories about the people who lived in those houses. – This will be the pride of Madrid—he said-. They've taken all of the little birds that used to live in the center of the city and they've come here, where they live much better. He told them many details about the houses, about the luxurious tearooms where the aristocracy entertained themselves. The middle-class housing, with food and furnished rooms, where the police never came; and the cheaper dining rooms, paradise for maids and poor soldiers, who couldn't hope for more.]

A little later, passing the point at which the Castellana began, the driver says proudly that "podemos seguir por aquí: por este sitio van a prolongar el paseo de la Castellana. Será el mejor paseo del mundo… ¡La felicidad de una parroquia!" [we can go this way: this is where they are going to prolong the Castellana. It will be the best road in the world… The pride of the town!] (1917: 111). As demonstrated in the previous chapter, *madrileños* in general knew quite a lot about the major urban plans due to the municipal government's widespread coverage of high-profile urban projects such as this one. Characters such as this coach driver voice a sense of awareness that these same projects were the government's means to stifle possible insurrection on the part of the urban population in the name of decreasing congestion. Early twentieth-century Madrid, with the Puerta del Sol at the center, would soon be altered by radical urban shifts. It is significant that during this drive with the discreet driver that Isabel's child is conceived. Both the city and the new child promise new opportunities, but both ultimately, the reader soon learns, come to a disastrous end.

The documentation of ways that female urban citizens found to survive on their own in the city make *La rampa* an unusual text for its time. There are moments of pleasure to be experienced in the city, distractions that arise both from technical innovations such as movies and from the grandeur of the theater and walks in Retiro Park. In a chapter entitled "Cinematógrafo" [Movie House], for example, Burgos writes about what it meant to young women to be able to go to the movies. For a time Isabel and Fernando go to see films every night of the week. This may seem excessive by today's standards, but the reason becomes clear in the following passage.

> Los cines eran un refugio de las parejas de enamorados vagabundos que se refugiaban en aquella sala de cine que ejercía tan gran atracción sobre ellos. Había una sugestión propicia para el amor. Algunas muchachitas iban allí solas con el deseo de correr aventuras. (1917: 94)

> [Movie theaters were a refuge for wandering love-struck couples who took refuge in the movie theater which held such a big attraction for them. There was a real promise of love in the air there. Some girls went by themselves wanting to find adventure.]

Even more enticing than the films themselves was the chance to sit in a comfortable, dark place which held the promise of sexual excitement. In this chapter Isabel begins to project herself onto the screen, relating to the silent film characters as if they were her contemporaries. Since she has had no previous experience with men, her budding relationship with Fernando is informed by the romantic scenes she witnesses on screen.

> La sensibilidad de Isabel, excitada por la vida de aislamiento y trabajo y encendida en su amor, sentía aquella influencia del cine que le hacía vivir, mezclada con sus personajes y con Fernando, las historias trágicas y amorosas del drama de la película. Encarnaba y veía encarnar a Fernando en aquellos personajes. Eran ellos mismos. Se veían como en un espejo, y aquella unión les hacía aproximarse más. (1917: 95)

> [Isabel's sensibility was so excitable because of her sheltered life and work. She was now overcome with love, and she responded to the influence of film because it made her feel alive and she combined the fiction-

al characters with herself and Fernando, and with the tragedies and love
stories of the film's plot. She saw herself and Fernando in those characters. They were the same. She saw herself as if in a mirror, and that connection made them even closer.]

Burgos eloquently narrates the capacity of film to influence women in
Madrid during a time of changing social values and gender roles. Her
wonder at the artistic possibilities of film are evident in the language
she uses to describe film spectatorship. Overall, though, Burgos criticizes what she sees as the negative influence of this most modern of
technologies on young women. The impractical role models present
in many of the films of the time provided an escape from the everyday
lives of many of the young women in the audience, but it is clear from
this chapter that Burgos, ever the didactic author and feminist,
thought that young women in particular took these glamorized,
romanticized images of modern women too seriously and that they
created myths that needed to be deconstructed with a critical eye.

At one point in the novel Isabel's life has taken a decidedly down-
ward turn: "Iba de prisa, empujada fatalmente por la rampa de su
vida" [She was quickly, fatally pushed down the ramp of her life]
(1917: 218). The last chapter hinges on a reference to the ramp of
the title: "Había llegado al final de la rampa ... definitivamente ven-
cida" [She had arrived at the end of the ramp ... definitively con-
quered] (1917: 249). The significance of the ramp as city street lies at
the center of the novel and provides for a polyvalent reading of what
can be thought of as an urban chronotope. The spatial connotation
of the road or city street is at once individual, collective and universal. Because the novel goes into great detail about the particularities
and concrete spaces of Madrid, this figurative and general use of the
ramp asks the reader to take this local knowledge and consider how it
functions on the grander scale of the international experience of
modern city life. Temporally, the ramp as the path of life asks the
reader important questions about the trajectory of one's life. The fact
that the ramp or city street is alternately seen as tilting upward for
some characters and downwards for others allows for a more open
reading of the book. Will Águeda achieve economic independence,

find support in her friends and enjoy the pleasures of the city? Will Isabel's solidarity with other women enable her to stand on her own again and recover from her personal loss? The answers lie on the street – the ramp – whose hidden histories and motives make the experience of living in the city a simultaneously exciting and unstable one.

The Place of Art and Commerce in *Los negociantes de la Puerta del Sol* and *El veneno del arte*

Another text capturing the urban experience in Madrid at the beginning of the twentieth century is *Los negociantes de la Puerta del Sol*, a novella which appeared in 1919, one year before the now better-known *Toda la Historia de la Puerta del Sol* of her collaborator and companion, Gómez de la Serna.[12] In *Los negociantes de la Puerta del Sol* Burgos describes the lives of recent migrants to the city—Don Justo, his wife Antonia, a son named Juanito and his daughter Anita, a family originally from the countryside. They are full of dreams of the economic prosperity they hope to attain through hard work. They soon find, however, that survival in the Puerta del Sol requires a hard-won knowledge of the intricate deception played out on the city streets. With the term "fetishism of commodities" Marx sought to capture the ways in which markets are created and goods are exchanged in a capitalist society obscure history and the true nature of social relations. In a similar fashion Burgos is interested in exposing the inner workings of the Puerta del Sol when she warns the reader, for example, that

> [N]o se puede uno fiar de nada en la Puerta del Sol, desde lo más grande hasta lo más sencillo. Existe la vendedora de periódicos viejos y atrasados, que los da como nuevos en el momento de subir el tranvía.

---

12. Núñez Rey and Castañeda both document the fact that Burgos and Gómez de la Serna wrote their books on the Puerta del Sol at the same time and shared their research on the history of the plaza with one another.

Hay la vendedora de alfileres que da un papel vacío y la que ofrece déci-
mos de lotería atrasados por el mismo procedimiento. (1989: 212)

[One can't trust anything in the Puerta del Sol, no matter how big or
how humble. There is a woman who sells old and out-of-date newspapers to people right as they get on the train, claiming that they are new.
There is a woman who sells pins but actually hands out empty pieces of
paper and who sells old lottery tickets the same way.]

The examples of the goods sold here highlight the ability of objects,
and language itself in the case of the newspaper, to obscure reality. If
people are sold out-of-date newspapers as they jump on the trolley in
the morning, they will read about a city that existed days ago.
Women will buy pins for sewing only to find when they arrive home
that they have been cheated and will not be able to do the work they
intended. False hope is sold in the form of lottery tickets that have
expired. Even money, that concrete abstraction of wealth, that which,
as Harvey puts it, "represents the greatest concentration of social
power in the midst of the greatest possible dispersal" (1985: 22) is in
this story being reproduced by counterfeiters in the back of a café
in the Puerta del Sol (1989: 211). Not only is honest work discour-
aged; it is practically impossible.

There are strong ties between the construction of place, urban
planning and the daily lives and experiences of individuals in this
work. Many streets in the neighborhoods off of the Puerta del Sol are
mentioned, as well as what one can expect to find there, from where
to go to Mass to where to find pornographic postcards and prostitutes. Pages 238-41 are no less than an itemized list containing
descriptions of the clientele, food and history of the most important
cafés in the area at the beginning of the century, such as the Correos,
Lisboa, Puerto Rico, Nuevo Levante, Universal, Montaña, Candelas,
Pombo, Colonial and Mayorquina. The text also relates historical
information about changes made to the Puerta del Sol. There is an
elderly friend of Don Justo's who tells the history of the plaza, looking back to the year 1909. The novel pays particular attention to
changes made between 1910 and 1918 and the *puertosolinos*'s reac-

tions to these changes. At one point Don Justo and his more histori-
cally-aware friend discuss the construction of the Gran Vía and voice
their concern that it will take away from what they understand to be
the centrality and splendor of the Puerta del Sol. They agree that

> El correo nuevo [referring to the Palacio de Comunicaciones by Ota-
> mendi and Palacios finished in 1917 at the beginning of the Gran Vía]
> debía haberse hecho allí [in the Puerta del Sol]. Eran los muchos enemi-
> gos de la Puerta del Sol—que también tenía amigos—los que pretendían
> llevarse el centro hacía allá. Pero no conseguirían nada. (1989: 249)

> [The new post office should have been put there. The Puerta del Sol had
> many enemies – who in turn had friends of their own – who tried to bring
> the center of the city elsewhere. But they wouldn't get anywhere with that.]

They could not be more wrong. The center of Madrid would shift.
Feeling superior because they live and work in the Puerta del Sol area
and considering themselves modern in the extreme out of a sense of
pride in their new home, these characters, like the worthless objects
sold in the Puerta del Sol, soon find themselves outdated, left behind
and betrayed by the modern urbanization process.

The novella begins with a description of a typical day in the Puerta del Sol.

> Más que el reloj del Ministerio de la Gobernación, marcaba las horas
> el aspecto de la gran plaza, que de hora en hora ofrecía un cambio
> notable. Era allí donde en las primeras horas de la mañana se percibía el
> bostezo de la ciudad que se despertaba y donde poco a poco iba afluyen-
> do la vida toda, como si cada una de las calles que conducen a ella fuesen
> los grandes ríos que reciben a su paso a todos los tributarios y van a
> desaguar en el océano de la Puerta del Sol, siempre revuelto y turbulento.
> Aquel barullo parecía que lo tonificaba, que había algo en la corriente de
> una gran muchedumbre que engendra una especie de energía eléctrica.
> Había sido siempre la Puerta del Sol el lugar más concurrido de Madrid,
> al que acudían todos aquellos arrieros y carreteros de las diferentes provin-
> cias de España, que entraban por la Puerta del Toledo a vender sus mer-
> cancías, cuando aún no había ferrocarriles. (1989: 205-206)

[More than the clock of the Government Ministry Building, the plaza itself kept time, because each hour there was a noticeable change. It was there that in the early hours of the morning you could witness the city's yawn as it woke up and from where little by little it spread everywhere, as if each one of the city streets that led into the plaza was a great river that had drawn water from many tributaries and flowed into the ocean of the Puerta del Sol, which was always teeming and turbulent. That racket seemed to buzz, and there seemed to be an energy that ran through the crowd like a type of electrical current. The Puerta del Sol had always been the most popular place in Madrid, where all of those mule and cart drivers arrived when they entered the city through the Puerta de Toledo to sell their goods, even before there were trains.]

From the very beginning, Burgos captures the centrality of the Puerta del Sol which, before the construction of the Gran Vía, was the focal point of the city and thus considered the geographic center of Spain itself. As outlined in Chapter Two, the Gran Vía was designed to draw congestion away from the Puerta del Sol and the surrounding areas. The first six pages of the text lay out the course of a whole day. There is a powerful sense of place, as already noted, but what Burgos does so skillfully here is to demonstrate how this place is linked to time. "La Puerta del Sol ha tenido siempre una relación con la hora" [the Puerta del Sol had always had a relationship to time] (1989: 223). The representation of the movement of the *puertosolinos* through both space and time humanizes what Harvey calls "the annihilation of space by time" (1985: 179): exactly how labor time defines money that in turn assures that time has a price, at once linking capital and space.

The great clock of the Government Ministry Building is ever-present and described in great detail. Just how important this clock is to Madrid's inhabitants is apparent when the narrator tells of a humorous occurrence on New Year's Eve.

Al dar las doce todos los ojos están fijos en el reloj, se inicia el movimiento de cansancio, en esa misa pagana al empezar a descender la bola. Es preciso no descuidarse en cumplir ese rito que asegura la felicidad de todo el año. Algunos quedan tristes y desanimados por no haber podido tomarlas lo bastante deprisa y un temor vago y supersticioso se

apodera de las almas. Es la verbena, la verdadera verbena, de la Puerta
del Sol, verbena sin farolillos, porque le basta solo para engalanarse el
prestigio de su reloj.

Un año la multitud esperó en vano: el reloj no dejó de caer su bola.
¿Se había descompuesto? Parece que eso era lo lógico pero el pueblo echó
la culpa a sus gobernantes y les achacó el hecho de amargar la alegría de
todo un pueblo en fiesta. Éste era un crimen. Había sido como matar-
los a todos … suspendiendo el tiempo y retardando la entrada del año.
(1989: 225-226)

[As it struck twelve all eyes were fixed on the clock, which began its
sleepy movement during that pagan mass that occurs when the ball
descends. It is important not to miss participating in this rite that assures
happiness for the entire year. Some people become sad and disheartened
when they haven't been able to participate and a vague and superstitious
fear overtakes their souls. It's the festival, the real festival of the Puerta
del Sol, a fair without lights because that would take away from the
clock's prestige.

One year the crowd waited in vain: the clock's ball did not descend.
Was it broken? That seemed the logical explanation but the crowd
blamed the government, attributing to it the poisoning of the happiness
of everyone at the celebration. This was a crime. It was like killing everyone … stopping time and delaying the New Year.]

The reaction of those celebrating New Year's Eve is one of disbelief
and betrayal. The clock has played a trick on them, making time
stand still. The municipal government is instantly blamed for the
catastrophe. The narrator's nostalgic tone communicates a sense that
there are some who wished that were the case, who longed for a previous epoch when time was not so directly linked to profit and everything moved just a bit slower. The chronotope of modernity created
here functions on symbolic, individual, community and national levels because of the many spatial and temporal connotations at play.

In the morning arrive the waves of recent immigrants and vendors
selling their wares. Later come the government officials, clerks, workers and housewives crowding the streets as they go about their daily
work.

Las paralelas se llenaban de obreros y empleados, ansiosos de tomar
su puesto en los tranvías, y las aceras se poblaban de la multitud que
pasaba de prisa, apresurada, en esa mezcla abigarrada de los elegantes y
los hombres de blusa, las mujeres de mantón y las de sombrero, los
mendigos y los chicuelos derrotados y astrosos con las gentes bien vesti-
das. (1989: 203)

> [The walkways would fill up with workers and clerks, anxious to get
> a place on the train, and the sidewalks were full of the crowd which went
> by quickly, in a hurry, in that heterogeneous mix of the elegantly and more
> humbly dressed, with women wearing expensive silk shawls and women
> wearing hats, beggars and ragged and dirty children with the best-dressed
> of people.]

While the narrator stresses social inequalities and the inherent dangers of living in the city throughout the novella, there is an exuberant
tone underlying the descriptions of the chaotic, fast-moving courses
taken by the lives of the inhabitants. The passage above denotes how
new means of transportation and communication have affected the
daily lives of individuals in Madrid, taking them to places they never
would have gone before, putting them side by side with a greater variety of their fellow *madrileños*.

There is an overall sense of nostalgia for the way the Puerta del
Sol used to be before Madrid began its modernization process. After
describing in detail some of the cries of the nineteenth-century street
vendors selling such things as chickens, eggs, cooking oil and vegetables, the narrator notes that the nature of the economy of the Puerta
del Sol has changed.

> Desaparecieron aquellas costumbres y aquellos tipos, dejaron de
> oírse aquellos gritos con sus diferentes tonos, pero todavía se vocea, se
> ofrecen mercancías y los vendedores ambulantes llenan la Puerta del Sol.
> No son ya vendedores de hortalizas, de quesos y de aceite, sino vende-
> dores de cosas que podíamos llamar *frívolas*, de un comercio más deli-
> cado. (1917: 205)

> [Some of those customs and archetypes disappeared, one stopped
> hearing them call out with their different tones, but there are still voices,

there are still merchandise and street merchants filling the Puerta del
Sol. They don't sell vegetables, cheese and olive oil any more, but things
that one could call *frivolous*, a more delicate business.]

Burgos is an astute observer of how the economy in the Puerta del
Sol begins to change as the city becomes more modern. When asked
to define her own style of writing, Burgos was often quoted as saying
that she was "una naturalista romántica" [a Romantic Naturalist].
This is a good description of the passages that describe the Puerta del
Sol here, since they demonstrate how social forces (such as modernization and urbanization) can have negative effects on individuals yet
she simultaneously engages in the nostalgic idealization of this environment. As in *La rampa*, Madrid between 1900 and 1930 is seen as
a fascinating place of adventure, movement and possibility for some,
while it can be a dead end or a trap for others.

The story ends with a description of what happens after the long,
scorching afternoon hours when the inhabitants of the Puerta del Sol
take their customary evening stroll.

> Y aquel reloj de la gente marcaba con sus manecillas gigantescas la
> hora de ir a cenar, dejando la gran plaza solitaria, con el suelo de luciente
> asfalto las luces movibles, los guardias a caballo en medio de la explanada.
> Marcaba la hora de ir a los teatros y la hora intermedia en que vendedo-
> res, golfos y muchachuelas reemplazaban la multitud elegante. Después la
> última ola de la salida de los teatros y las silenciosas horas de la madru-
> gada, en las que lucía la torre del reloj en la soledad y la sombra que agran-
> daban la plaza, que simboliza el centro de España, el corazón de Madrid,
> cuanto hay de más neto y castizo en la capital del reino, la corona de esa
> capital. (1989: 206)

> [And the people's clock indicated when to eat dinner with its giant
> hands, leaving the plaza empty, with the moving lights on the shining
> asphalt, the soldiers on horseback in the middle of the esplanade. It kept
> track of what time to go to the theaters and that in-between time when
> street merchants, beggars and young girls took the place of the more ele-
> gant crowd. After the last wave of those exiting the theaters and the silent
> dawn hours when the clock tower shined in its isolation and the shadow

that took over the plaza that symbolizes the center of Spain, what is there more pure and typically Spanish in the capital of the country, in the crown of the capital.]

While much attention is paid to the history of the physical structure of the plaza, the narrator of the text is primarily interested in the overwhelming waves of humanity ruled by the clock that dictates what happens and when. There is a strict order and predictability to the chaos due to the structure of the buildings, streets and means of transportation that organize people into their daily activities. While many of the inhabitants of the plaza are compassionately portrayed as caught in difficult circumstances, the symbolic use of the ebb and flow of the streams into the vast ocean of the plaza implies that one's fortune can turn like the tide, so to speak—that there will be new opportunities and circumstances every day in the city. The Puerta del Sol at the beginning of the twentieth century that we see in *Los negociantes de la Puerta del Sol* is a microcosm of the city just beginning to feel the effects of modernity. The centrality of the clock makes the Puerta del Sol seem like a small village with its collective life centered on the Church and its bells. Life on the Gran Vía, as we will see in the next chapter, would be radically different.

The novella is curious due to its use of several very different narrative styles. The text begins with a detailed and seemingly objective history of the Puerta del Sol. Indeed, the chief protagonist is the place itself. The detailed history is not just the story of the construction and destruction of buildings, however, but the course of human events that is contained by the physical space. *Los negociantes*, the most modernist of the three Burgos texts discussed here, is divided into twenty-two fragments of varying length, a structure that lends itself easily to jumps in time and a capacity to abruptly change the point of view from which the plaza is observed. The *puertosolinos* are divided into a complex web of picaresque groups that seem to treat the plaza as their only home. (In the case of some of them who are homeless, this is quite literally true.) The impression created by the narrative representation of this dense area populated by many different and competing but nevertheless interdependent groups is that of a nucleus of the capital itself.

There is a secondary plot, although following it is not central to the success of the novella as a piece of literature. It involves the loss of innocence of a country bumpkin who is taken for everything he has upon arrival to Madrid and how he, over time, manages to learn the rules of the game in order to survive in the Puerta del Sol and eventually become one of its residents. Don Justo gives money to an "executive" of a made-up company called Ramírez y Compañía, an outfit supposedly involved in a get-rich-quick scheme to extract gold from the bed of the Manzanares River. When they first arrive, the family seems sure they will be part of a great modern initiative bringing prosperity to all. For example, the son Juanito "participaba de las ilusiones de su padre al que veía volver cada noche lleno de una alegría nueva, de una esperanza reanimada en los estupendos negocios que podían hacerse en 'este país' donde estaba 'todo por hacer'" [shared in the illusions of his father who would come home each night full of a new happiness, of a rekindled hope in the stupendous business that they could do in 'this country' where 'everything was about to happen'] (1989: 222). After Don Justo and Juanito realize they are being swindled, they go through a long, difficult process of reevaluation during which "Don Justo veía ya la mala fe de los vendedores, engañando al público con drogas que carecían de las virtudes que ellos les atribuían" [Don Justo now understood the bad faith of the street merchants, fooling the public with drugs that lacked the virtues that were attributed to them] (1989: 241). By the end of *Los negociantes de la Puerta del Sol* the painful and humiliating process of initiation into the metropolis is complete. Don Justo becomes a true *puertosolino* by hanging a shallow box on his neck and spending his days selling a brand of toothpaste that supposedly cleans one's teeth without the need to use a toothbrush. In Burgos's words: "Esta vez Don Justo labraba su fortuna sólidamente. Su conocimiento del espíritu nacional lo había salvado y sobre todo su fe y su amor a aquel centro de la Puerta del Sol que absorbió su vida toda" [This time Don Justo was solidly in control of his earnings. His knowledge of the national spirit and even more his faith and love for that center of the Puerta del Sol that absorbed his entire life are what saved him] (1989: 259).

One year after the publication of *Los negociantes de la Puerta del Sol* Burgos published *El veneno del arte*. Full of autobiographical references, this short novel was a reflection on the author's intellectual and personal development since her arrival in Madrid almost twenty years earlier. As such it criticizes the bohemian cultural scene in which she participated in Madrid during the first two decades of the twentieth century. Almost all of the characters are thinly-veiled references to actual figures. The one character whose actions run the course of the work is the Count Luis de Lara, who represents Antonio de Hoyos y Vincent, a writer, aristocrat and active member of the intellectual circles of Madrid who was at the center of a long-running *tertulia*. Like *Los negociantes de la Puerta del Sol*, there is a plot but it is secondary to the stream of ideas, opinions, and descriptions of the narrator. In *El veneno del arte* Burgos rallies against the small world of artists, writers and hangers-on who, in her opinion, spend all of their time engaging in false, pretentious conversation in cafes instead of doing anything truly creative or productive.[13] She presents almost all of them as "provincianos que llegaban con su caudal de ilusiones, dispuestos a luchar" [country boys who came with an abundance of illusions, ready to struggle] (1989: 223) who "vivían muriendo, sin dinero, sin comer," [lived dying, without money, without eating] (1989: 223) who find it necessary to prove they are artists "con las largas melenas y en el descuido de los trajes comprados en el Rastro," [with their long hair and the disheveled suits they had bought at the Rastro] (1989: 223) while others "intentan ocultar sus zapatos rotos y americanas raídas" [try to hide their worn shoes and old jackets] (1989: 223). "La mayor parte de ellos tenía la idea de que para vencer era preciso hacer una vida canallesca" [Most of them thought that

---

13. See Bellver and Mangini. Rosa Chacel, though much younger than Burgos, documents the experience of attending some of the most important café *tertulias* in the 1920s in Madrid. She found the experience unproductive and alienating. Burgos's solution to this problem was to form her own *tertulia* in her home, which for a number of years was extremely influential and well attended.

one was successful if one led the bohemian life] (1989: 224). These young "artistas sin arte," [artless artists] (1989: 239) as she calls them, "no tenían paciencia para estudiar y trabajar produciendo una gran obra" [did not have the patience to study and work to produce a great work of art] (1989: 240). What really bothers the narrator is their lack of social awareness or concern. She calls their type of rebellion "palabra muy socorrida a pesar de su falta de ideales sociales o humanitarios" [lip service because of their lack of social and humanitarian ideals] (1989: 240). Alongside these young (pseudo)intellectuals, Burgos places and comments on the critics of the time. She denounces the practice of condemning that which they haven't read, those who judge "con el argumento español 'porque sí'" [with the Spanish argument 'just because'] (1989: 247).

Burgos herself had actively participated in this café society of bohemian rebellion which may have had some authentic moments for her but was more often a form of posing. One of the most interesting aspects of *El veneno del arte* is that Burgos satirizes herself along with her companions. She is the nameless young woman, the feminist writer, "de ampuloso decir" [full of herself and what she has to say] (1989: 252), whom some of the young men call "Emperatriz de las cursis" [Empress of the pretentious] (1989: 252). She presents an earlier version of herself as somewhat of a pest, repeating over and over the same idea to her fellow writers: "¡Cuánto podía hacer un hombre de su talento por las reivindicaciones del bello sexo!" [The feats that a man of such talent would perform in order to stake a claim on the fair sex!] (1989: 253). Burgos represents herself as a headstrong, somewhat fanatical young woman from the countryside, poorly dressed and hungry, "con su libro místico de moral de cocina, dedicado a la condesa madre [Emilia Pardo Bazán] a la cual llamaba 'protectora de las artes' y 'portaestandarte del femenismo'" [with her mystical book of cuisine and morality dedicated to the mother Countess whom she called 'protector of the arts' and 'standard-bearer of feminism'] (1989: 253). The tone is very important because the reader senses that Burgos sees her past enthusiasm and ignorance from a great distance because she has come so far, greatly changed her attitude and direction and established herself as a professional writer and activist. Despite this self-criticism, Burgos still maintains the Krausist convictions she brought with her two decades earlier from Andalusia, as is apparent when she says "[Y]o tengo fe en los jóvenes sensatos que leen, trabajan y estudian" [I trust in the sensible young men who read, work and study] (1989: 261). Several times she talks about the need for a secular education, attacking Spain's Jesuit educational traditions and institutions.

This narrator has a love/hate relationship with Madrid and the places that make these types of new cultural exchanges possible. Hers is an attitude that permeates almost everything written by Burgos about the city, as can be seen in the discussion of the two works above. "Madrid es un villorrio donde todos nos conocemos y la gazmoñería impera…. Todos los selectos huyen de aquí…. No es posible tratarse más que con tal o cual viejo ridículo, chulos … escritorzuelos hambrientos y toreros de menor cuantía…. Todos explotadores" [Madrid is a one-horse town where we all know each other and hypocrisy rules…. The cream of the crop flee from here…. You can do no more than deal with this or that ridiculous old man, rogues … hungry minor writers and little-known bullfighters …. All smooth operators] (1989: 270). She immediately continues, however, saying that "vuelvo a Madrid con la nostalgia de todos los madrileños, ávido de respirar en nuestra Moncloa, de ver la Puerta del Sol y la Cibeles… No hay como Madrid en el mundo. Las demás ciudades sirven para una temporada, en Madrid, la vida" [I return to Madrid with the longing of all *madrileños*, anxious to breathe in the air of our Moncloa, to see the Puerta del Sol and the Cibeles… There is nothing like Madrid in all the world. Other cities are fine for a short time, but Madrid is for life.] (1989: 271). Madrid's modernity is seen as provincial, local, and faltering. But Burgos embraces it in the end because it is her own and she knows how to move through its spaces with expertise. Unlike in *La rampa* and *Los negociantes*, the city is conceived of in this work as a whole. There is a conspicuous lack of attention to geographical place and little differentiation between neighborhoods and the roles that people have in differentiated space. Because the short story creates a false "scene," the geographical and spatial relationships are vague and dream-like.

In her article "Modernidad y femenismo" Rodríguez shows that in *El veneno del arte*

> [S]egún relata la narradora … el arte se presenta como una forma de envenenamiento para los jóvenes que llegan a Madrid y que se dejan fascinar por las apariencias, rehuyendo el arduo estudio y la preparación que la autora estima necesarios para alcanzar el éxito…. Cargados con las nuevas connotaciones de la reproducción, el arte contamina y envenena. (1997: 389)

> [According to the story that the narrator tells … art is seen as a type of poison for the young people who come to Madrid and let themselves be fascinated by appearances, rejecting the long and difficult study and preparation that the author considers necessary for the attainment of success…. Weighed down with the new meanings of mass reproduction, art contaminates and poisons them.]

Burgos, some years older than most of the almost exclusively male artists and writers who were to make up the modernist and avant-garde art scenes of the 1920s, never could fully embrace their lifestyle or cultural values. A person formed chiefly in the nineteenth century, she belongs right at the beginning of the truly modern period in Madrid, a precursor to the avant-garde that would later draw its inspiration from everything new. Her work, although at times decidedly influenced by the broader modernist and avant-garde movements, never ceased to comment clearly and forcefully on Spain's social and political problems. Her writing, after all, was conceived for the marketplace and sold exceedingly well at the same time that it sowed seeds of contestation and dissent while often drawing special attention to the situation of women in the city.

The burgeoning capitalism of modern, industrial Madrid in the first two decades of the twentieth century was an urban, revolutionary mode of production of goods and of culture. It sought tirelessly to form new forms of organization, new technologies, new ways of life, new modes of production and exploitation, and new social spaces in which men and women could live. Madrid offered Burgos a space where on a personal level she could become independent, and where she could attempt to change the role of women in Spanish society as a writer and activist. The city, however, as we shall see over and over again in this study, is capable of creating a false image of itself that hides the reality of the experience of the majority of its inhabitants. The extremely detailed descriptions of the lives of the everyday people who populate Burgos's novels and short stories as well as her personal, eclectic and oftentimes passionate style, resulted in some of her contemporaries thinking of her as a frivolous author too focused on women's issues. It is true that her many narrative representations of Madrid at the beginning of the century were somewhat different from that of her contemporaries. Her ideas about industrialization, progress and cultural production are almost always concerned with the female experience, which she consistently finds limiting. There is no doubt that the capital was a place of relative freedom and liberation for her in that she broke through many barriers for women. Her writing, however, went into great detail about both the promises and dangers the city had to offer women looking to follow in her shoes.

CHAPTER IV

José Díaz Fernández's *La Venus mecánica:* Modern Fashion and Gendered Spaces

> That which withers in the age of mechanical reproduction is the aura of the work of art…. One might generalize by saying the technique of reproduction detaches the reproduced object from the domain of tradition. By making many reproductions it substitutes a plurality of copies for a unique existence. And in permitting the reproduction to meet the beholder in his own particular situation, it reactivates the object reproduced. These two processes lead to a tremendous shattering of tradition which is the obverse of the contemporary crisis and renewal of mankind. Both processes are intimately connected with the contemporary mass movements. (1968: 233)
>
> WALTER BENJAMIN,
> *'The Work of Art in the Age of Mechanical Reproduction'*

Much like Simmel in the first issue of the *Revista de Occidente* discussed in Chapter One, Benjamin describes the desire to purchase and subsequently identify with a mass-produced item that simultaneously isolates and legitimizes the buyer. This tension between the individual and the collective, this confluence of object and subject, in its urban context, makes up the nature of twentieth-century mass movements and the consumption of culture in the broadest sense of the word. The twentieth century has repeatedly been characterized as the age of the masses and the city is, after all, the location where those who decide what is fashionable live and work, and where the capital necessary to launch and advertise mass-produced objects is concentrated.

Theorists of the fashion industry claim that the characteristics of mass society have been unavoidably imprinted upon twentieth-century clothing and impacted our attitudes toward dress and identity.[1] Advances in the technology and materials used for clothing production have undoubtedly provided more comfortable, cheaper and attractive items to a larger proportion of the population, while the mediums through which fashion change has been communicated have allowed for an equally wide dissemination of fashion information and broader opportunities for the stimulation of a more homogeneous public imagination. The fashion magazine and the Hollywood film in particular brought fashionable models to a hugely expanded audience from the 1920s onwards, material examples of their dream peddling often made available through the expansion of chain stores and mail order companies. At the same time, paradoxically, a reorganization of business practices of marketing and advertising prioritized particular strands of society as fashion leaders. A cult of the designer revolving around ideas of *haute couture* and high fashion coexisted with strong subcultural identities, resulting in contrasting notions of quality, style, and individuality. As Jennifer Craik comments:

> The new approach to fashion was schizophrenic. On the one hand, fashion was democratized as more people had access to the images and clothing preferred by the trendsetters. On the other hand, fashion producers were setting the styles. Other changes were also occurring in the fashion industry. The aristocracy was supplanted as the elite fashion community and role models. Socialites, artists and movie stars offered

1. The study of fashion has become a rich area of research and interpretation in the last twenty years. Formerly the province of museum curators and theatrical designers, this area has been opened up by a variety of academic disciplines, from anthropology to sociology. Authoritative sources for general theoretical approaches and historical information are Barnard, Breward, Hollander and Lipovetsky.

alternative sources of inspiration. These role models offered desirable images and behaviors that were no longer based on emulating one's superiors. Individualism and modernity prevailed. (1994: 74)

Without a doubt, the promise of the "new woman" was linked to utopian images of the modern metropolis in graphic design, film and fashion trends. This chapter investigates the relationship between fashion in particular, mass culture in general and the urbanization of consciousness in Madrid in the 1920s as found in José Díaz Fernández's 1929 novel *La Venus mecánica*.

Women as Icons of Modernity in 1920s Madrid

A discussion of fashion and style in the twenties runs the risk of falling into generalizations. It was a period of rapid fashion change and very different, overlapping styles. The "ideal modern woman" of the 1920s in Spain looked dramatically different from the types of women described by Carmen de Burgos in the 1910s. The flat, geometrical, boyish forms so often associated with feminine dress of the decade made no real impact until approximately 1926, and then the cropped hair and knee-length skirts were confined to an elite and metropolitan market, or the abstracted illustrations of magazines and advertisements.[2] Before World War One, fashionable style tended toward a statuesque, heavy-chested look, hips thrown back and accentuated with flared skirts, or the alternative thin skirt.[3] There are very differing

---

2. Gronow analyzes the aestheticization of everyday life and studies the effects and causes of the wider dissemination of fashion information. Because different socio-economic groups have different tastes, taste is an empirical category. One of the main theses of her book, in her words, is that 'one cannot understand the modern consumer society and the meaning of consumption in a modern society if the social mechanism of fashion, a self-dynamic social process, is not properly understood and analyzed' (1997: xi).

3. See Barnard for the reasons behind the shift from the corset to the use of the mass-produced brassiere. He adheres to a 'theory of the shifting erogenous zone' wherein a culture's sexual interest in the female anatomy continually shifts

opinions as to whether the turn-of-the-century look was more comfortable for women than that of the flapper of the 1920s. In terms of
practicality and comfort, the earlier look was perhaps preferable to the
chest-denying rubber corseting and sweaty man-made fibers of the later
twenties. However, as Lola Gavarrón points out, due to women's collective liberation from the corset, "la mujer que se anuncia en los años
veinte recuerda ya la figura humana. Ha recobrado los movimientos
humanos. Es, por fin, un ser humano" [the woman advertised in the
1920s starts to look more like a human figure. She has recovered her
ability to move. She is finally a human being] (1982: 232). The truth of
the matter may lie somewhere in between. The vast majority of women
in the 1920s and 1930s did not wear impractical flapper-inspired clothing, although their wardrobes did begin to include more close-fitting
clothes that included details and designs inspired by men's fashions.[4]

For the average consumer, however, the impact of late-'20s fashion on anything more than surface appearances was more limited.
Elizabeth Wilson suggests a more circumspect reading of its importance in terms of female emancipation:

> The standard interpretation of the fashions and customs of the
> 1920s is precisely this: to translate short skirts, cosmetics and cigarette
> smoking directly into 'freedom' for women. As in the 1960s, the situa-
> tion was actually more complex and more contradictory. The popular
> meaning of 'emancipation' for women had shifted away from the ideas
> of social and political rights that had been so important before 1914.

---

from one part to another, 'now the chest, now the behind, now the legs and so on'
(1996: 54-55).

4. Hollander argues that no matter how similar the clothes of men and women
appear, or how different, the arrangements of each are always being made with
respect to each other. In her words, 'male and female clothing, taken together,
illustrates what people wish the relation between men and women to be, besides
indicating the separate peace each sex is making with fashion or custom at any
given time' (1994: 7). She sees the history of fashion as a duet between men and
women, sexuality being visualized in clothing and divided in modern times into
two main categories: male and female.

Social emancipation—the freedom to drink, to smoke, even to make love, to dispense forever with chaperones—served as a substitute for possibly more solid economic freedoms, and was in any case an option only for those few women who were socially and economically independent. (1990: 34)

In material terms the allure of modern women's fashion was beyond the reach of most. Few in the 1930s could afford new clothes at all. Mothers, sisters and friends usually put together copies of these clothes with material they bought or from inexpensive department stores that only vaguely resembled the designer's originals.

Recent work on dress and the body, formulated from a Cultural Studies perspective, has been useful in highlighting the way that the media form constructions of class, gender and sexuality.[5] Unfortunately, this work has sometimes been at the expense of historical specificity. A careful look at the popular magazines of Madrid in the 1920s and 1930s brings to light a relatively sudden democratization of fashionability due to advances in clothing technology, a further expansion of the publicity and advertising machines to incorporate film, radio and mass-circulation periodicals, and a perceived broadening of employment and educational opportunities for women and the working class. At first glance, one is left with a simplified and overly glamorized image of the twenties' fashionable female, swathed in Chanel, sunburned on the tennis court, reclining leisurely and answering to the name of flapper, a literal reflection of the advertising expertise of Hollywood and *Harper's Bazaar*. There were magazines published in and for the inhabitants of Madrid that were very similar

---

5. One of the most significant contributions of feminist film theory and visual studies has been the existence of the concept of the image of woman as a construction. As this argument goes, the image is a product of culture in several senses at once—as it has been industrially manufactured, as it has been pieced together according to aesthetic rules, and as it has been prefabricated by men. The image of woman, as this argument continues, is exactly what it is only because of the society which creates it, and in order to alter this image, we have to reconstruct that society. See Gaines and Herzog.

to magazines like *Vogue* and *Harper's Bazaar* in the United States and
La Vie Parisienne in France. [6]

One magazine, the very successful *Blanco y Negro* founded in
1891 by Luca de Tena, is of great importance to the study of mass
urban culture in Madrid. In the 1920s, the magazine proffered an
image of women increasingly active in all aspects of urban society
and constructed a new, radically different feminine stereotype. Human
reactions to an increasingly urban, modern, capitalist system are
played out in the pages of *Blanco y Negro*.[7] One sees visual references
to new systems of relationships and hierarchies. There is a crisis of
traditional values, incipient consumerism, the eruption of very different fashions in clothing and lifestyles, certain sexual, class and racial
taboos are overcome or at least questioned, and what is introduced is
a secular attitude that counters Spain's traditionally Catholic outlook.
Significantly, women are almost never portrayed in the private space
of the home but in the city street or participating in athletic activities. (*Fig. 4.1*) Almost all of the illustrations of women include either
the backdrop of an urban cityscape or leisure activity that takes place
in the countryside or at the beach. A high percentage involves women in
cars, trains, boats and automobiles. This was a purely bourgeois revolution of social values, but the inaccessibility of this lifestyle to the
vast majority *Blanco y Negro*'s middle-class readers did not impede
the magazine's success.

---

6. Gavarrón acknowledges the particular importance of the fashion magazines *Miss*
    and *Chic* in her history of women's underwear in Spain (1982: 235-244).
7. This urban chaos resulting from political turmoil and the need for social change
    is depicted in the visual arts throughout the first three decades of the twentieth
    century. 'The Mechanical Paradise,' the first chapter of Hughes's *The Shock of the
    New* shows that at the turn of the century until World War One, technology was
    seen as promising emancipation from excessive labor and a thing of beauty in
    itself. After 1914, however, 'machinery was turned on its inventors and its chil-
    dren. After forty years of continuous peace in Europe, the worst war in history
    cancelled the faith in good technology, the benevolent machine. The myth of the
    Future went into shock, and European art went into its years of irony, disgust,
    and protest' (1991: 56).

Francisco Javier Pérez Rojas points out the following in his introduction to a collection of images of women from *Blanco y Negro*:

> La mujer va a ser presentada como símbolo de esta nueva sociedad y mentalidad transformada, como prueba de la liberalización emprendida en una nueva época en la que caen mitos y conceptos vitales ancestrales.... Usos más propios de *cocottes* lo adaptan las burguesas y aristócratas y ahora resultan *chic*. Pero todos esos cambios y rupturas se desenvuelven en un marco estrictamente urbano y en unos ambientes sociales muy minoritarios que son los que en gran medida reflejan los ilustrados gráficos, los cuales los afrontan con ironía y humor en creaciones donde se viene a criticar la doble moral burguesa. (1997: 16-17)

> [Women would be presented as symbols of this newly-transformed society and mentality, as proof of the liberalization of the new age in which vital myths and concepts were losing all authority. What before were used by *cocottes* were now used by the middle class and aristocrats and made *chic*. But all of those changes and ruptures took place in a strictly urban environment and in very small minority social groups that to a large extent reflected the graphic illustrations, where the double standard of middle-class morality was treated with irony and humor.]

Some of the reasons behind the portrayal of the strong, independent, sensual woman are economic. Magazines such as *Blanco y Negro* created a new market for products in Madrid. Their new values and role in society seemed to require new clothes, shoes, perfumes, cosmetics, new fashions for hair, even a new, slimmer body shape. (*Fig. 4.2*) Images of this new woman dominate the movie screens and are also presented in the form of the art deco-inspired *femme fatale* or urban vamp.[8] In the face of this stream of images of independent women as

---

8. Wilson explores the relationship of fashion to art in the 1920s. 'The fashions of the 1920s, for example, cannot just be interpreted (as they usually boringly are) as expressive of women's emancipation and a new sexual freedom. That was all happening before the First World War—Paul Poiret, the revolutionary French designer, abandoned the corset in 1904' (1990: 33). More significant, in Wilson's eyes, are the urban motifs in fashion that stem from movements such as modernism

athletes, airplane pilots, university graduates, professionals and social and political progressives, feminists like Margarita Nelken likewise warned that this independence was relative:

> Lo que no puede esta mujer española, a quien la Naturaleza 'madura' mucho antes que a la escandinava o a la anglosajona; lo que no puede esta mujer, que tal vez es ya abogada, ingeniera, doctora en medicina, es, antes de los veinticinco años, viajar cuando lo estima conveniente sin permiso de sus padres o tutores. Lo que no puede es, hasta los veinticin-co años ... disponer libremente de su persona.... Y el enmendar esa ley nos parece bastante más decisivo, en cuanto a emancipación, que el acce-so a las carreras liberales. (1922: 176)

> [What this Spanish woman cannot do, who Nature 'matures' much earlier than the Scandinavian or the Anglo-Saxon woman; what this woman cannot do, even if she is a lawyer, engineer, medical doctor, is, before she is twenty-five years old, travel when it is convenient for her to travel without the permission of her parents or her tutors. What she can-not do is, before she is twenty-five years old ... be free to behave as she pleases.... And revising this law seems much more decisive to us, in terms of emancipation, than access to professional opportunities.]

The joyful, breezy exuberance of many of the proud, free women in the images of *Blanco y Negro* may have had a grain a truth in them. They must be tempered by a dose of reality, however. The dreamy portrayal of these wealthy, independent women appealed to women and men alike in no small part because they were worlds away from their own personal realities.

Fashionable women are at home on the big city street in the draw-ings of the most important graphic artists like Enrique Varela de Sei-jas, Loygorri, Ramón Manchón, Joaquín Valverde, Rafael de Pena-

---

and futurism: '1920s fashion imitated aspects of modernism in featuring abstract designs and in rendering the body as two-dimensional and flat as possible. They were futurist in suggesting the speed and the clean lines of the machine' (1990: 34). Huyssen's 'The Vamp and the Machine' is another influential essay on this topic.

gos, Federico Ribas, Roberto Martínez Baldrich, Salvador Bartolozzi and Ramón Roqueta, all of whom worked and lived in Madrid but whose work rarely depicted local scenes. Neither do the women look particularly Spanish. Their city backdrops are the generalized metropolises of work and leisure, movement and glamour. The magazine's writers and artists supplied their readers with what they demanded: a model of life that seemed always fresh, new, avant-garde and exciting even if just out of reach.

Fashion in particular and the modern image business in general thrive precisely because styles change. Fashion drawing of the twenties and later fashion photography of the thirties, in Hollander's words, "emphasized the dependence of desirable looks on completely ephemeral visual satisfaction, the harmony of the immediate moment only, which exists totally and changes totally, shifting to the next by no visible process" (1994: 163). While fashion may be the costuming for a glamorous urban theater, it is a problematic means of expression that runs the risk of alienation. It is precisely this two-sided nature of fashion in its urban context that José Diaz Fernández outlines and criticizes in his 1929 novel.

Díaz Fernández and *El nuevo romanticismo*

Biographer Víctor Fuentes describes José Díaz Fernández as "uno de los hombres más representativos de una juventud intelectual que acudió a su cita con la historia" [one of the most representative of the young intellectuals who was brave enough to shape history] and situates him with "aquellos jóvenes intelectuales procedentes de la pequeña y media burguesía, la otra generación del 25 o 27" [those young intellectuals who came from the middle class, the other Generation of '25 or '27] (Prologue to *El blocao* 7). Born in Aldea del Obispo (Salamanca) in 1898 and raised in Asturias, Díaz Fernández studied law at the University of Oviedo before moving to Madrid. He participated in the colonial warfare in Morocco from February of 1921 to August of 1922. He was stationed during this time in blockades in Tetuán and Beni Arós where he participated in some skirmishes. His overall experience was one of boredom, which he chronicled in his first novel, *El blocao* (1928). Upon returning to Gijón after his military service, Díaz Fernández accepted an offer to work at the prestigious Madrid newspaper *El Sol* as a literary correspondent. Once in Madrid, Díaz Fernández met and worked with other like-minded intellectuals interested in both politics and literature. Like them, he was interested in literature from outside of Spain, mostly the novel of the Russian revolution by such authors as Gladkov and Leoniv, the German pacifist novel of authors such as Gleser and Zweig and writers of the United States' "Lost Generation" such as Dos Passos, Steinbeck and Hemingway (Fuentes 1980: 71). Díaz Fernández participated in many student demonstrations in Madrid and founded several magazines, including *Post-guerra*, [Post-War] "una revista de vanguardia política y literaria" [an avant-garde political and literary magazine], considered one of the first serialized publications in Spain to identify the avant-garde approach to literature as being one containing a radical social and political potential.

Towards the end of 1928, Díaz Fernández and several others (among them Joaquín Arderíus, José Antonio Balbontín, Giménez Siles, Juan de Andrade, Graco Marsá and César Falcón) founded Ediciones Oriente, one of many small left-leaning publishing houses that cropped up during this period. They decided to publish books instead of magazines and journals because they saw this as one way to avoid censorship laws which had authorized the printing of books of more than two hundred pages without previous approval by a censor. At first they simply translated social novels from outside of Spain, but when the success of these grew beyond their expectations, they decided to start a separate series called "Historia Nueva" [New Story/History], dedicated to Spanish and Latin American authors. The first publication in this series was Díaz Fernández's *El blocao* *[The Barracks]*. [9] The novel was an immediate success. The book was

---

9. Published in 1928, a year after the Annual disaster, *El blocao* spoke directly to what Díaz Fernández in a prologue to the second edition of the novel called 'una herida abierta en la conciencia española' [an open wound in the Spanish

translated into English, French and German and received very favorable reviews. Díaz Fernández began working with a group called Acción Republicana which was outlawed by the government in 1928. As a result he went to jail for three months in Madrid's Modelo Prison and was exiled for three months in Lisbon, from February to September of 1929. It is during this six-month period that he wrote *La Venus mecánica*. [10]

With Antonio Espina and Adolfo Salazar (who was soon after replaced by Joaquín Arderíus) Díaz Fernández founded and co-edited the magazine *Nueva España*, which at its height in 1930 reached 40,000 readers. The stated intent of the magazine was to be "el órgano de enlace de la generación de 1930 y el más avanzado de la izquierda española" [the organ that linked the Generation of 1930 and the most advanced of the Spanish Left]. The 1930 publication of Díaz Fernández's *El nuevo romanticismo. Polémica de arte, política y literatura* [*The New Romanticism. A Polemic of Art, Politics, and Literature*] is considered a major turning point in the development of the social novel in Spain in the 1930s. It is here that the author responds directly to Ortega y Gasset's 1925 *La deshumanización del arte* and *Ideas sobre la novela* with a call for the politicization of art, or what he called "el nuevo romanticismo del hombre y la máquina que harán un arte para la vida, no una vida para el arte" [the new Romanticism of man and machine that will make an art for life, not a life for art] (1930: 45). When *El Sol* fell into the hands of the monarchy, Díaz Fernández and others abandoned the newspaper and went on to

---

consciousness]. Themes seen in *El blocao* which are apparent again in *La Venus mecánica* include brutal violence against women, the difficulty of forming meaningful relationships in a modern world (especially between men and women), and the evolution of human beings into a well-organized social machinery devoid of any real thought or emotion.

10. Boetsch and Santonja agree that Díaz Fernández stopped writing fiction after the publication of *La Venus mecánica* because he doubted the power of his words to further political change in Spain. It does seem significant that after the publication of this novel, Díaz Fernández only writes political articles and biographies of revolutionaries until his untimely death in 1941.

found the more radical *Crisol y Luz*, which lasted only a year. Díaz Fernández was elected representative to the national Cortes by the Radical Socialist Party in 1931, and became part of the legislative body of the Second Republic for two years. It is also in 1931 that he, together with his friend Arderíus, published *La vida de Fernán Galán*, a biography of the anarchist leader who fought against the monarchy. It was in the last two years of the Second Republic that Díaz Fernández began to work on the newspaper *El Liberal*. Under the pseudonym José Canel, he published *Octubre rojo en Asturias*, a narrated account of the armed Asturian insurrection of 1934. Running as a member of Manuel Azaña's Partido Izquierda Republicana in 1936, Díaz Fernández was elected congressional representative to Murcia. When the Civil War broke out in 1936, Díaz Fernández was named "Jefe de Prensa" [Press Chief] in Barcelona, where he lived with his family. He occupied this post until January of 1939, when he fled to France for safety. After spending time in a concentration camp, he was released and returned to his family in Toulouse in 1941, where, while awaiting safe passage on a boat to Cuba, he died of a pulmonary infection in February of 1941.[11]

La Venus mecánica

La Venus mecánica takes place in Madrid toward the end of the dictatorship of Primo de Rivera. More than just a backdrop, though, the city as cultural and political capital and the experience of a very diverse group of individuals in this specific place add to the fragmented feel of the novel. The author pieces together historical and fictional events in true avant-garde fashion, which permits him to comment on avant-garde art and popular culture, Spanish politics, and the behavior of the Spanish bourgeoisie in a time of crisis. As outlined in Chapters One and Two, the years 1928 through 1936

---

11. Trustworthy biographical information on Díaz Fernández can be found in Fuentes (1980: 82-90) and Boetsch (1985: 14-20).

were historically tumultuous, a moment in which the substitution of
the Second Republic controlled by the moderate Left for the monarchy created an environment that was more open to the social realist
novel after a decade when avant-garde literature flourished. [12]

The novel has two main protagonists: Obdulia, a young woman
from a middle-class family that has fallen on hard times, and the
young, middle-class journalist Víctor, who in many respects represents Díaz Fernández himself. There are three main themes. The first
is the problematic role of the bourgeois intellectual (Víctor) who
becomes active in the revolution of the proletariat. The second is the
equally problematic position of young women (Obdulia) who look
for independence and freedom in an urban environment that nevertheless remains dangerous and closed to them. The third is a harsh
critique of avant-garde culture. Geographically, the novel belongs
almost exclusively to the Gran Vía. These three themes are played out
on the major boulevard as they are increasingly intertwined towards
the end of the novel when the alienated Obdulia and Víctor reconcile
their initially frustrated relationship. All three themes hinge on the

---

12. Santonja and Esteban refer to Díaz Fernández's 1930 *El nuevo romanticismo* as

> un libro absolutamente clave, de lectura imprescindible, que generó amplia
> y apasionada polémica. Desde sus páginas el autor abogaba por la vuelta a
> la realidad, haciendo de lo humano en contenido primordial del arte y colo-
> cando al servicio de este afán la depurada técnica vanguardista, cuyo estilo
> trepidante y fragmentario consideraba el más adecuado para reflejar la pro-
> blemática de la sociedad moderna, pero poniendo muchísimo énfasis en
> denunciar los peligros que supondría elevar dicha técnica a la categoría de
> objetivo final. (1987: 11)

> [an absolutely essential book that must be read – one that generated a wide
> and passionate polemic. From its pages the author argued for a return to
> reality, making humanity the primordial content of art and using the puri-
> fied avant-garde techniques at his service, whose vibrant and fragmented
> style he considered the most adequate to reflect the problems of modern
> society, but placing much emphasis on denouncing the inherent dangers of
> elevating said technique to the category of a final objective.

same dilemma, voiced by Víctor: "Pero es que no sé si soy individualista o colectivista" [The thing is that I don't know if I am an individualist or a collectivist] (1929: 87). The end of the novel testifies to the saving power of the true, committed love relationship (though significantly still outside of marriage), the identification with society at large and concern for the working class as opposed to what Díaz Fernández saw as the bourgeois values and avant-garde aesthetic of the time. Obdulia and Víctor, after a series of difficult personal experiences, eventually grow together and decide to take revolutionary action. In the very last phrases of the novel, Obdulia goes to the Modelo Prison where Víctor has been incarcerated to tell him that their infant son has died.

> —Cuando salgas, yo te ayudaré a preparar nuestra venganza.
> Venganza. Venganza. Qué bien sonaba la palabra allí, bajo las bóvedas sombrías, bajo el techo ingrato y polvoriento. La boca de Obdulia parecía morderla como un fruto, el único que rueda, verde y apetecible, por el piso de todas las cárceles. (310-11)

> [When you get out, I will help you to prepare our revenge. Revenge. Revenge. The word sounded so good there, under the shadowy ceiling of the vault-like prison, under the unpleasant and dusty roof. Obdulia's mouth seemed to bite the word like a piece of fruit, the only one to roll, green and appetizing, around the floor of every jail.]

The reified word spoken by Obdulia strengthens, inspires and unites both characters. In a similar fashion, Díaz Fernández wrote his novels of political and social critique in order to affect his readers and motivate them to act politically. It is only after they are forced out of the false and decadent forms of modernity to which they contribute in their previous lives on and around the Gran Vía that they can make these solemn vows to each other in the subterranean jail cell.

La Venus mecánica includes the voices of a variety of narrators who speak in the first, second and third person. At times these voices speak in a measured, objective manner which, aside from maintaining the linear progression of the plot, describe daily life, the political situation and social conflict in the streets of Madrid. However, unlike the prototypical realist novel and unlike the Burgos texts analyzed in the previous chapter, *La Venus mecánica* is subjective. Díaz Fernández includes a more pensive, introspective stream-of-consciousness interspersed with more realistic, objective language to discuss the general sensation and experience of life in Madrid in the 1920s, to great effect. Díaz Fernández's fiction lies somewhere in between the traditionally-demarcated realms of the social and the avant-garde novel. [13]

A look at the cover of the first edition, designed by graphic artist Ramón Puyol, informs the reader of its avant-garde tendencies. (*Fig. 4.3*) With its Cubist representation of the image of a nude woman further depersonalized by the metal grating on the bottom left, the wheel and the road on the right and the grim, primitive figure of the male spectator on the top right, the book's cover skillfully encompasses the main themes of the novel. The novel's persistent, specific and detailed attack on gender and economic inequality and political corruption in the specific context of Madrid in the 1920s locate it squarely within the category of the social novel. Only a handful of literary critics and historians such as Fulgencio Castañar and Laurent Boetsch have placed Díaz Fernández and (other authors such as Ramón Sender, Andrés Carranque de Ríos and Joaquín Arderíus) at the intersection between these two literary currents. Díaz Fernández can be credited for drawing on the avant-garde and combining it with what the social novel as a genre had to offer in order to initiate a new literary movement in Spain.

La Venus mecánica is the concrete application of the theories found in *El nuevo romanticismo*, and Díaz Fernández's portrayal of

---

13. Herzberger finds in *El nuevo romanticismo* an important theory of narrative that lies between what he calls 'the metonymic pole of discourse' or the belief that language can reflect life as it really is, and 'the metaphorical pole of discourse' or the concept that language can reflect nothing except its own creation. He calls Díaz Fernández's theory a reconciliation that 'turns upon a modified version of the reflection theory of literature, which takes into account the necessary split-referential functioning of the language of literary discourse' (1993: 85).

Madrid in the 1920s is significantly informed by the non-representa-
tional avant-garde techniques that he uses. Thematically speaking,
his critique of avant-garde culture focuses on what he sees as its lack
of political involvement and awareness. At the same time, as a writer,
he finds avant-garde literary techniques very conducive to writing
about the modern city. This original and genre-bending text seems
the written embodiment of what Lefebvre outlines in his aforementioned theory of social space. The author locates the ideological
positions of two of Madrid's citizens – the middle-class radicalized
intellectual and the young woman with no family attachments and
no money – to compare and contrast their very different experiences
of the same built environment. The two protagonists reflect on these
positions (what Lefebvre called the *perceived* and the *conceived*), and
their radically different urban identities grow closer and closer
together through a process of rejecting many of the myths created by
imaginative representations of the city until at the end of the novel
the two create their own way of resisting urban hegemonic power
(what Lefebvre called the *lived*).

The division of *La Venus mecánica* into 45 short chapters gives the
novel a fragmented, unsettled feel that does its best to capture the
competing discourses found in the freely circulating forms of high
and low culture in the city. Víctor and Obdulia speak about themselves in the first person, but there are also chapters where an omnis-
cient narrator describes their situations and activities. The narrator
tells of the trials and triumphs of random city dwellers who seemingly have no connection to the main plot. There are selections that con-
sist of letters between Obdulia and Víctor, obituaries such as that of
the dancer María Mussolini, lectures such as the one given by the
Ayn Rand-like American proto-Fascist Miss Mary in the Hotel Gran
Vía, moralistic newspaper editorials and personal diaries worked into
the text that provide for a wide variety of voices and perspectives on
life in modernizing Madrid. One moment the object of the narrative
descriptions is the city as a whole and is seen from a distance while in
the next the reader is looking into the minute and very personal

details of one of the city's inhabitants. The reader is called upon to piece together these narrative threads and assorted descriptions however they can. Like the elegant, walking fashion plates on the covers of *Blanco y Negro* mentioned earlier, seen from afar, the city is dynamic, exciting and full of promise. A closer look at the lives of the fictional characters, however, gives the reader quite another impression.

The young and fashionable Obdulia is characterized throughout the novel as a woman trapped within the social and economic barriers of her time. She is portrayed not as a human being but as a "mujer-mercancía" [merchandise-woman], as the "Venus mecánica" [mechanical Venus] of the title. The unnamed narrator of Chapter 13 (entitled "Capítulo para muchachas solas" [Chapter for Single Women]) briefly sketches the lives of women such as Obdulia, painting them as works in progress and as inevitable products of the modern city:

Algún día ha de llegar en que no existan esas muchachas perdidas, indecisas, que merodean alrededor del bar económico donde han comido alguna vez. No se atreven a entrar porque en el fondo de su bolso no hay más que la polvera exprimida, la barra de carmín, sangrienta y chiquita como un dedo recién mutilado, y la factura sin pagar de la última fonda. Muchachas de zapatos gastados y sombreros deslucidos, que buscan un empleo y terminan por encontrar un amante. Un pintor actual podría retratar en ellas la desolación de una urbe: al fondo, la valla de un solar; a la izquierda, un desmonte, y más lejos, la espalda iluminada de un rascacielos. (1929: 93).

[Some day in the future those lost, indecisive girls who wander around the cheap bar where they ate once will no longer exist. They don't dare to enter because at the bottom of their bags there is nothing more than pressed powder, a lipstick, small and bloody like a recently-mutilated finger, and an unpaid bill from their last meal. Girls with worn shoes and ruined hats who look for work and end up finding a lover. A painter would be able to capture in them the desolation of a city: in the background, the barrier of an empty plot of land waiting to be built upon; to the left, a clearing and, further off, the illuminated spine of a skyscraper.]

The dynamic, youthful excitement of the city street is influenced by and in turn influences the young women who have flocked to Madrid looking for work, forming new versions of themselves based on images of the feminine they see in other women, store windows, the popular press and film.[14]

To elaborate on this one need look no further than the title of the novel, as it is an obvious reference to the modern fabrication of women described above. In this image of the title are synthesized youth, eroticism and the mechanical, three characteristics that the avant-garde saw as being positive and desirable. When Obdulia is described in these terms, however, the reader understands them to be quite problematic. In fact, the development of Obdulia's character involves her increasing strength to fight off the burden of being the "Venus mecánica." She is forced to grow up quickly in an environment where her body is the only thing she has to offer in exchange for the money she needs to survive. The "mechanized" aspect of the woman of the title suggests a dehumanization which certainly applies to Obdulia during the first half of the novel. It is gradually worn away as Obdulia adopts more of an awareness of how society has forced her into her situation, a personal and political resistance to this society and, most of all, an identification with the underprivileged.

The reader first meets Obdulia in the cabaret of the Teatro Alkázar, where she works as a "tanguista," dancing with men for a fee with the promise of sexual favors after hours (1929: 40-54). It is clear that she rails against the situation in which she has found herself. "Es

---

14. Felski and Huyssen have written about the changing status of women under conditions of urbanization and industrialization. Felski states that this socio-economic change 'expressed itself in a metaphorical linking of women with technology and mass production. No longer placed in simple opposition to the rationalizing logic of the modern, women were now also seen to be constructed through it' (1995: 20). Along the same lines, Huyssen describes how the effects of industry and technology serve to demystify the myth of femininity as the last remaining site of redemptive nature and how, paradoxically, the figure of the woman as machine can be read as a patriarchal desire for technological mastery over women.

que aborrezco esta vida. No me acostumbro. Cada vez que entro allí siento un frío en las entrañas..., pero eso era lo de menos. Lo peor era tener que devorar mis pensamientos" [I abhor this life. I can't get used to it. Each time I come in here I get chilled to my core..., but that was the least of it. The worst thing was having to get rid of my thoughts] (1929: 56). The thoughts to which she refers are of the circumstances that have brought her to this point in her life–namely, the economic downfall of her previously stable middle-class family. Her father, ashamed, abandons the family. Her mother tries to force Obdulia to marry a policeman she finds unbearable (in no small part because he is her mother's lover), and Obdulia runs away to find her own way in the world. Like *La rampa*, there is much of the typical serialized romance novel here, with the young, beautiful, hard-working, well-intentioned heroine being abandoned to a cruel world until she cleverly manages to redeem her situation by hooking a rich man who will save her from certain doom and launch her into a safe, bourgeois existence. Díaz Fernández paints a different picture, however. The rich man in *La Venus mecánica* is not Obdulia's salvation but her cross to bear, as she gets pregnant by him. Obdulia then decides to sacrifice her comfortable existence with the wealthy mine owner for her uncertain love for the journalist, Víctor. By the end of the novel she vows to change her world by unselfishly engaging in revolutionary activities. Her liberation comes from an evolution from her comfortable but solitary existence to solidarity with Víctor and the revolutionary ideals they share.

Obdulia is not an individual case in *La Venus mecánica*. Díaz Fernández mentions other women in similar situations, abandoned to their own devices to survive in a world where they are forced to sell the only thing they have—themselves. The death of the dancer nicknamed María Mussolini found at the center of the somewhat abstract chapter mentioned above, causes in Obdulia "una indefinible pesadumbre ... una angustia difusa e indeterminada de vivir, una sensación abstracta de riesgos, y pesares futuros, una inquietud oscura y humana" [an indefinable grief ... a diffuse and indeterminate living anguish, an abstract sense of risks and future sorrows, a dark and human unsettled feeling] (1929: 84-85). Another woman in similar circumstances is the diva Asunción Lanza, who "tenía fama de mujer áspera, caprichosa, y colérica que sufría con frecuencia crisis espirituales" [was famous for being tough, capricious, and hot-tempered, who went through frequent spiritual crises] (1929: 122-123). When she is followed across the country by a former lover who is significantly younger than herself, she unselfishly decides that it would be a mistake to encourage him, reasoning that

> Lo cierto es que a los cuarenta años todos los sentimientos, todas las palabras, todos los instintos están gastados. ¿Para qué seguir? Si yo fuera una mujer como muchas, te haría presa de mis nervios, de mis caprichos. Eres tan ingenuo y tan impetuoso. No, no – me voy para no verte más, para que la vida se ensanche en torno suyo. (1929: 126)

> [The truth was that at forty years of age all of the feelings, all of the words, all of the instincts are used up. Why go on? If I were like other women, I would make you a prisoner of my nerves, of my whims. You are so naïve and so impetuous. No, I'm leaving and won't see you anymore, so that life will go your way.]

These secondary female characters, serving as foils for the fuller development of the fictional Obdulia, together make up a critique of the new, modern woman described in the beginning of this chapter. Not satisfied with the appearance, the mystery and promise of sexual adventures that these women supposedly offer, Díaz Fernández seeks to locate these modern notions of femininity within their urban contexts.

The way in which Obdulia ultimately achieves her freedom is both significant and problematic. As she becomes more liberated she suffers a conflict surrounding her relationship with Víctor. She is concerned that the relationship makes her dependent on him and is not consistent with her ideas about what it means to be a liberated woman, the woman she wants to be:

> Ella [Obdulia] quería trabajar, ganarse la vida como una obrera, como una de aquellas muchachas de los talleres y las oficinas que cruzaban en grupos alegres la Puerta del Sol. Y se resistía a confesarle a Víctor

su pobreza, su debilidad, porque así se vería disminuida, insignifican-
te.... Si su amor tenía que apoyarse en él, recibir protección y consuelo,
¿qué era lo que daba ella, gota de azar, tímido grito de la desigualdad
humana? (1929: 89-90)

> [She wanted to work, to make a living like a worker, like one of those
> shop and office girls who crossed the Puerta del Sol in happy groups.
> And she resisted telling Víctor about her poverty, her weakness, because
> he would see her as being less, insignificant.... If their love had to be
> supported by him, receive protection and consolation, what did she have
> to contribute, belittled by fate, a timid cry of human inequality?]

The only way Obdulia can resolve this conflict is to definitively reject
bourgeois society altogether. When Víctor and Obdulia declare their
revolutionary intentions, the inequality between them disappears and
they both feel free for the first time.

Part of Obdulia's problem is that her middle-class background
impedes her from being able to truly belong to the working class, to
"ganarse la vida como obrera" [earn her living like a worker]. She feels
her only recourse is to prostitution, to become a plaything for the
very rich, to become the embodiment of the "Venus mecánica." It is
precisely when she makes this decision that the critique of the idealized modern woman is strongest. The Jazz Age "new woman," in
Spain and elsewhere, is a superficial creation, a woman who represents herself in a shroud of mystery—her clothing, her beauty, her
looks creating a playful image of herself to be looked upon with
admiration. Díaz Fernández takes it upon himself to describe this
type of woman, but from the inside, where the truth behind the elab-
orately made-up façade is strikingly different. In one of the most
important passages of the novel, we hear in Obdulia's words one
account of how it feels to play this role:

> Yo, Venus mecánica, maniquí humano, transformista de hotel, tengo
> también mi traje favorito, mi elegancia de muchacha que sabe vestir para
> la calle, para el teatro y para el 'te dansant'. Conozco el color que arrastra
> a los hombres y el que impresiona a las mujeres. Finjo que voy a las carre-
> ras, que he de cenar fuera de casa o que salgo de compras por la mañana,

después de las doce, bajo el arco de cristal de los barrenderos. Soy una actriz de actitudes, una pobre actriz de trapo, que no puede siquiera llevarse las manos al corazón para hacer más patético el verso que dicta el apuntador. (1929: 117)

[I, the mechanical Venus, human mannequin, hotel chameleon, I also have my favorite suit, the elegance of a girl who knows how to dress for the street, for the theater and for the private dance. I know which color attracts men and impresses women. I pretend that I'm going to the races, that I am going to eat out or that I go shopping in the morning, after noon, under the crystal arches of the arcade. I'm an actress of different attitudes, a poor actress in rags, who can't even bring my hands to my heart to make the line that is fed to me by the prompter any more pathetic.]

Here the modern Madrid in which Obdulia lives is the stage for her performance, a demeaning one where her role is imposed on her and leaves no room for self-expression or meaningful communication with others. It is at this point in the novel that she is just beginning to be able to articulate her sense of injustice and throw off the values of middle-class society that seek to silence her completely. Having had enough of being the object of desire and her body being used as merchandise, given over for the pleasure of others again and again, she finally reclaims it for herself.

Obdulia's journey from prostitute to fashion model to kept woman over time instills in her a strong hatred of the society which has used her in these ways. She fails as a prostitute because she cannot submit herself to the anonymous eroticism of the trade. She screams at her first client: "Te odio.... Os odio a todos. Al mundo también... Qué desgracia" [I hate you.... I hate all of you. The world too..... What a disgrace] (1929: 105). As a model, the conformity and boredom of bourgeois life and tastes and the lack of meaning of the fashion industry and life in general overwhelm her. At one point she thinks to herself: "¿Qué derecho tienen sobre mí las mujeres que triunfan, ésas para quienes trabajo? Yo no me resigno" [What right do these successful women, the ones for whom I work, have over me? I can't get used to it] (1929: 133). At one point early in the novel

Obdulia is fooled into thinking she will become a film star. She quickly realizes that the woman who claims she is producing a film (Esperanza Brul) is a con artist/poseur only interested in the favors granted to her by those who hope to participate in said films. Esperanza's desire for Obdulia becomes obvious when Obdulia is made to come back repeatedly for screen tests that never seem to amount to anything. Bitter and desperate, Obdulia decides to let the married, wealthy mine owner don Sebastián support her but only because she very consciously wants to make him suffer. She sees this as the only way to fight the system that has destroyed her. Obdulia derives no real power from this relationship, however, as it ends poorly for her when she becomes pregnant by don Sebastián, a man she detests. She returns to Madrid out of desperation.

As don Sebastián's lover, Obdulia represents luxury, "ácido corruptor de la riqueza, venganza de todos los desheredados de la tierra" [the corroding acid of wealth, and the vengeance of the underprivileged] (1929: 14), according to Díaz Fernández. Paradoxically, Obdulia's experience with the wealthy man is an important part of her consciousness formation which leads to her eventual liberation. When she visits one of don Sebastián's mines, she enters "un mundo distinto, el del esfuerzo muscular, el de la esclavitud asalariada" [a different world, that of strong muscles, that of wage slavery] (1929: 156). She cannot but help feel solidarity with the men, women and children working in the mines and feels rage against Sebastián for causing such injustice. In the end, though, love for herself wins out over her hatred of Sebastián. Obdulia returns to Madrid, initially avoiding contact with Víctor. When she finds out she will have Sebastián's child, however, she is devastated because "ella no quería un hijo de la esclavitud, un hijo del odio, concebido en tinieblas. Quería un hijo del amor, sembrado en su corazón primero que en su carne, un hijo a quien habría de enseñar a aborrecer la injusticia y amar la libertad y el talento" [she did not want to have a child born into slavery, a child of hatred, conceived in darkness. She wanted a child born of love, planted in her heart even more than in her body, someone she could teach to erase injustice and love liberty and talent] (1929: 217). She returns to Víctor, who helps her obtain an abortion in France. Díaz Fernández implicitly defends the right of a woman to an abortion primarily because it is what allows Obdulia to take back the possession of her own body. As the doctor performing the operation in Paris tells her, "Nuestro cuerpo es ya lo único que nos pertenece" [our body is the only thing that belongs to us] (1929: 190).

Víctor and Obdulia begin a new relationship and their love initially seems to conquer all obstacles. When they both want to have a child of their own, Obdulia feels that finally, this child "puede justificar de algún modo mi paso por la tierra, mi paso trémulo que no acaba de atravesar la frontera de los deseos" [can justify somehow my walking the Earth, my tenuous steps that never stop crossing the boundaries of my desires] (1929: 256). Obdulia sees in the birth of her child the opportunity to erase the trials and mistakes of her own life and to prepare him to be free and strong. The death of the infant, therefore, signals the unfairness and uncertainty of life. After this personal tragedy Obdulia has to once again face her prospects in life, this time free of any vestiges of the bourgeois society such as marriage and family. At the very end of the novel it is Obdulia who proposes to her jailed lover Víctor that they act as revolutionaries to change the society in which they live. It is significant that Obdulia does not find the support she needs in any of the feminist movements going on around her, but rather through her own experience. She decides her destiny for herself. As Boetsch points out, "ella sólo ha logrado sobrevivir en una sociedad corrupta e injusta por haberse deshumanizado. Sin embargo, se impone en ella la conciencia de que esa injusticia es más general que su propio caso, de que se trata de una injusticia social colectiva de la cual ella es parte" [she only manages to survive in a corrupt and unjust society by having become dehumanized. Nevertheless, she becomes conscious of the fact that it is a collective injustice of which she is a part] (1985: 121).

There is an inherent problem in the portrayal of Obdulia's fight against patriarchal, bourgeois oppression, however. The only way out of her situation is tied to the economic prospects and professional stability of a man, namely Víctor. This unresolvable problem is seen throughout Díaz Fernández's *El nuevo romanticismo* (1930), the first chapter of which is entitled "La moda y el femenismo" [Fashion and

Feminism], and where he complains "la sociedad es manca, porque le falta el brazo activo de la mujer" [the body of society is incomplete because it lacks the active arm of woman] (49). While Díaz Fernández is obviously concerned about the limited opportunities for women in Spanish society, he has no real solutions to propose. On the contrary— he furthers values that subjugate women by condemning the suffragist movement on the basis of its being run by upper-middle class women. While it is important to note, as Díaz Fernández does in his essays, articles and novels, that women unable to compete in the workplace with men due to lack of education and opportunity should be considered an underprivileged class, he dismisses feminism as a consciousness-raising movement in its 1920s form. He writes in *El nuevo romanticismo* that "nuestras damas del movimiento feminista están todavía tan retrasadas que siguen pidiendo para la mujer el voto político y el escaño parlamentario" [well-to-do ladies of the feminist movement are so backward that they continue to ask for women's right to vote and to run for parliament] (1930: 16). Deploring the lack of education for women is defending them. Denying their right to participate in representative, democratic government is further confining them to their subordinate position in modern society. This inherent contradiction in Díaz Fernández's social theories works its way into and problematizes the evolution of characters such as Obdulia into more mature, self-actualized women in *La Venus mecánica*.

Víctor Murias is the second protagonist who, like Obdulia, is corrupted by the city around him and goes through a series of dramatic changes that culminate at the end of the novel in a resolution to act with a social conscience. Víctor is a thirty year-old journalist, the prototype of the privileged but radicalized intellectual of Díaz Fernández's generation. Going back and forth between the different spaces of Madrid, Víctor is the perfect witness and commentator on the many different types of modern urban experiences of Madrid during the 1920s. In the first half of the novel Víctor seems to live in two very different, mutually exclusive worlds. In one, he writes pointed criticism of Madrid's middle class and avant-garde art, he collaborates on revolutionary manifestos and attends meetings where he participates in planning the overthrow of the dictatorship of Primo de Rivera. In the other, he is the decadent young man in pursuit of fleeting erotic experiences which at first seem liberating but become more and more meaningless and emotionally damaging. Through the figure of Víctor, Díaz Fernández critiques the behavior of the young bourgeois intellectual, who, as Obdulia says of Víctor when she firsts meets him: "vive fluctuando entre el escepticismo y la acción, como corcho entre dos olas" [lives fluctuating between skepticism and action, like cork between two waves] (1929: 90).

The very first pages of the novel describe how Víctor has a way of chasing after women that belittles both him and the women he admires from afar. Víctor loathes himself for acting this way, but cannot seem to help himself. At one point he describes himself as "ese hombre de guardia a las puertas de una tienda, ese mendigo de palabras y sonrisas fugaces, ese misógino devorador de citas falsas y respuestas equívocas que desgasta su alma en todos los quicios y todas las esquinas" [that watchman in the doorway of a store, that man begging for words and quick smiles, that misogynist consumer of false dates and lying responses who wastes away his soul on every corner] (1929: 11).

Although his relationships seem to end only in frustration, Víctor cannot seem to help but get erotically involved with a series of different women.[15] A sharp observer, intelligent and good-looking, there are many literary allusions to him as a consumer of female bodies. At one point Víctor describes the young women of Madrid as being

> más que mujeres, esquemas de mujeres como las pinturas de Picasso. Pura geometría, donde ha quedado la línea sucinta e imprescindible... En realidad, aquella figura no era ya un producto natural sino artificial... Era una sutil colaboración de la máquina y la industria, de la técnica y el arte. Alimentos concentrados, brisas artificiales del automóvil y el ventilador

---

15. Edith Kaisor, the German countess with whom Víctor shares a true friendship, is the only exception.

electrónico, iodos del tocador, sombras de cinema y claridades de gas...
Esa mujer... es hija de los ingenieros, de los modistas, de los perfumistas,
de los operadores, de los mecánicos. (1929: 19-20)

[more than women, outlines of women like those in the paintings of
Picasso. Pure geometry, where the concise and most basic lines
remain.... In truth, that figure wasn't a natural but an unnatural one....
It was a subtle collaboration of machine and industry, of technology and
art. Concentrated food, artificial automobile and electric fan breezes,
chemical concoctions from the dressing room table, cinema shadows
and radiator steam.... That type of woman ... is the daughter of engineers, of fashion and perfume designers, of telecommunications opera-
tors, of mechanics.]

Díaz Fernández here documents the "new woman" made not of flesh
and blood but of geometry, film, aura and clothing–all combined to
produce an image of the modern woman as product, in the most literal sense of the word, in Víctor's case. It is against this synthetic,
superficial, dehumanized quality that Obdulia struggles throughout
the novel, trying to find an escape from an upper class that considers
this new type of woman to be a positive product of new technologies
and social values. One of the original traits of *La Venus mecánica* is
the way it describes–from both sides of the exchange–how human
beings relate to one another within an increasingly market-driven,
image-conscious, urban setting.

When Víctor meets Obdulia and falls in love with her, he begins
to try to overcome his previous attitudes towards women. From the
very first time they meet in the cabaret of the Teatro Alkázar, Obdulia
interests Víctor for reasons that are not purely sexual. Víctor realizes:

Obdulia sí era una muchacha interesante. Tendría unos veinte años y
sus ojos eran negros y hondos.... Me dejo vencer por la imaginación. Es
una mujer vulgar. Un poco bonito, pero vulgar. Y me parece que se trata
de una mujer de excepción.... Estoy hecho un idiota. (1929: 48-51)

[Obdulia was obviously an interesting girl. She must have been
about twenty years old and her eyes were black and deep.... I let my

imagination go. She's a common woman. Somewhat pretty, but common. And it seems to me that she is an exceptional woman.... She's made me into an idiot.]

When Víctor falls in love, he does not entirely stop pursuing other women, but his encounters with them become increasingly absurd and pathetic. He begins to think of them as belonging to the same underprivileged class as Obdulia. Indeed, the descriptions of these other women serve to flesh out what the reader knows about the life of Obdulia, and to point to the fact that Obdulia is not alone in having to resort to prostitution. While sexual freedom was seen as symptomatic of true rebellion and liberty for many in the 1920s, in *La Venus mecánica* it is seen in a negative light. In search of new values for his generation, Díaz Fernández values love and fidelity over the erotic for its own sake. This conflict is central to the development of Víctor's character.

In a similar vein, the evolution of Víctor's political thought follows a trajectory from closed self-absorption to a more collective, open mindset that allows him to see the big picture and join forces with the working class in opposition to the dictatorship. When Víctor asks himself "Pero es que soy individualista o colectivista; si quiero la disciplina o el desorden" [Whether I'm a loner or a joiner; if I want discipline or disorder] (1929: 254) the reader senses that Víctor is at a turning point. He is a well-educated young man living in a time of intense social and political upheaval. He feels some responsibility as a man of privilege and a journalist to help in the push for a more progressive society, but is uncertain as to how he should act since he is not a member of the ruling class per se. His discussions with his good friend Doctor Sureda (whose character is based on the figure of Gregorio Marañón) clearly demonstrate where Víctor stands intellectually in terms of the revolution (Fuentes 1993: 41). He comes to the conclusion that there is a need for the intellectual to understand and respect the masses, to give in to them, no matter what the cost. When Sureda recommends political reform, Víctor responds with an emphatic

no, querido doctor. Lo que hay que hacer es provocar la gran revolución. Ustedes se empeñan en soslayar el problema, en confeccionar fórmulas pacíficas, sin contenido humano. Y mientras, el pueblo quiere otras cosas, se muere de esperanza por otra cosa. (1929: 190)

[no, my dear doctor. What one has to do is to start the revolution. You manage to sidestep the problem, to come up with pacifist solutions, with no human content. And meanwhile, the people want other things, they are dying of hope for something else.]

It is through his journalism that Víctor eventually becomes part of the revolution. When the general strike occurs, Víctor works day and night to inform the Spanish public of exactly what is going on, from a revolutionary perspective. "En aquel momento, más que periodista, se sentía colaborador del proletariado combatiente" [At that moment, more than a journalist, he felt like he was collaborating with the fighting proletariat] (1929: 266). Víctor finally realizes and furthers a cause that is much greater than himself. When he is put in jail for his publications and the son in which he had put so much hope for the future dies, his revolutionary fervor does not diminish.

Estos días han servido para enardecerme. Hasta ahora yo no sabía lo que era el dolor. Pero advierto que el dolor no puede conmigo. Obdulia, amor mío, me encuentro más dispuesto que nunca. (1929: 310)

[These past few days have served to inspire me. Until now I did not know what pain was. But I warn you that pain will not conquer me. Obdulia, my love, I'm more ready now than ever.]

Víctor's revolutionary attitudes and values evolve quite differently from those of Obdulia, however. Throughout most of the novel his point of view is from above, literally out of the window of the Gran Vía Hotel and figuratively as an economically stable member of Madrid society. His revolutionary fervor stems from an individual reaction to his difficult personal situation, not from any real solidarity, understanding or contact with the working class. His response to the revolution is mostly intellectual. It is Obdulia who, willingly or not, is thrust into the day-to-day hardship of the struggles for power going on in the streets of Madrid, not Víctor. Her role as "la Venus

mecánica" and, as a woman, her subordinate position as an economi-
cally-disadvantaged person informs Víctor of to the day-to-day struggle for survival of the rest of Madrid society, but he never can fully
share in it.

Gendered Redefinitions of Urban Space

There is a very strong sense of place in *La Venus mecánica* that contrasts sharply with the abstract urban space of the sort depicted in the
magazine *Blanco y Negro* mentioned above (*Fig. 4.4*). Dozens of specific locations and streets are mentioned so the reader knows precisely
where the fictional characters live and work. The novel even mentions the specific addresses of many of the characters which gives the
reader a sense that they are being taken on a guided tour of the spaces
where the novel takes place and that the novel seeks to capture a fleeting moment in the rapidly-changing city.[16] *La Venus mecánica* begins,
tellingly, with a disjointed exchange between Víctor and an anonymous woman with whom he tries to talk as she is getting into a taxi.
It is quoted at length here to give a sense of the rhythm of the prose,
as well as the type of language used and the themes presented. What
follows is a confusion of sounds, sights, emotions, memories and
rapid displacements from one place to another along the Calle de
Alcalá and the Gran Vía.

> ¿Qué género de memoria era la suya que en su fondo turbio sentía
> estremecerse, en desconcertante confusión, partículas de recuerdos y
> larvas de presentimientos, residuos de pasado y átomos de futuro? ...
> Víctor fue de nuevo, un instante, ese hombre de guardia a las puertas de
> una tienda, ese mendigo de palabras y sonrisas fugaces, ese misógino

---

16. See Davidson for a different reading of two spaces in *La Venus mecánica:* the
hotel and the cabaret. Davidson sees these spaces as potentially alienating but
ultimately rehumanized – this rehumanization linked to the social purpose of
the novel.

devorador de citas falsas y respuestas equívocas que desgasta su alma en todos los quicios y todas las esquinas. Por eso, para desquitarse, cuando la desconocida salió con sus paquetes, la afrontó decidido hasta incurrir en la burla del chófer.

Pero, en fin, esa mujer ya no existía. Se había diluido como una gota azul en el torrente urbano de las ocho de la noche. Cruzó la calle de Peligros y salió a la Gran Vía, casi contento de encontrarse otra vez con su libre albedrío, lejos de la complicación amorosa que desbarataba sus horas y le tenía semanas enteras alejado su trabajo. (1929: 9-10)

[What kind of memory did he have, that deep, turbulent memory he felt trembling, in disconcerting confusion, pieces of his memories and larvae of his premonitions, leftovers from the past and atoms of the future? … Once again Víctor was, for an instant, the man who keeps watch over the store entrance, begging for a word and a fleeting smile, that misogynistic consumer of false appointments and false answers that exhausted his soul on all fronts and on every corner. That is why, to get even with her, when the unknown woman left with her packages, he decided to confront her even if it would incur the mockery of the chauffer.

But, in the end, that was gone. She had disappeared like a blue drop in the urban torrent of eight in the evening. He crossed Peligros Street and went out to the Gran Vía, almost happy to once again find himself with his own free will, far from the amorous complications that cheapened his hours and kept him for weeks from his work.]

We learn from this passage that Víctor is a young, handsome, stylish man in the habit of pursuing and ultimately charming so many women that he can no longer differentiate between them. The problem is that their individual features are so confused in his mind, the encounters so brief, that he can remember no one woman in her entirety. They appear in the narrative here as the figures in the Cubist paintings of Picasso, an artist the narrator specifically mentions. The constant coming and going of unaccompanied women shopping along the Calle de Alcalá and the Gran Vía provide an insurmountable temptation to him, and he waits and watches for them regularly. He is, in effect, consuming them, choosing certain women over others for their color, shape, smell, and overall style just as the women shopping for fashion and beauty products are doing, constructing an ongoing cycle of consumption and production based solely on desire. This desire for satisfaction, whether it be sexual or for ownership of the latest, most fashionable of objects is rampant in *La Venus mecánica* and goes hand in hand with the urban experience. It is only when Víctor and Obdulia step outside of this system that they are able to find a way to live more authentic and fulfilling lives.

The experience of the center of 1920s Madrid is captured here, to great effect. There is a sensation of the coexistence of the past, present and future which forms a key part of Víctor's experience of the city and the reader's experience of the novel. Because many women who shop in this part of town look the same because they wear the same kinds of clothes, he cannot remember if he has met the particular woman mentioned here. When Víctor asks, "¿Qué género de memoria era la suya que en su fondo turbio sentía estremecerse, en desconcertante confusión, partículas de recuerdos y larvas de presentimientos, residuos de pasado y átomos del futuro?" [What kind of memory did he have, that deep, turbulent memory he felt trembling, in disconcerting confusion, pieces of his memories and larvae of his premonitions, leftovers from the past and atoms of the future?] (1929: 9-10) Díaz Fernández uses pseudo-scientific terms to get at the nature of the protagonist's urban consciousness. Víctor's inability to focus on any one woman as a person and his incapacity to put together series of events that have happened to him in the past are presented as problems to the reader and disconcerting dilemmas for the protagonist, who at one point in his journey from the bottom to the top of the Gran Vía stares at a store window, "sin mirarlo, distraído con aquel rompecabezas interior" [without seeing it, distracted by that interior puzzle] (10). The unseeing Víctor feels numbed by the rapid movements of the taxis and trams, the crowds of strangers and the mechanical precision and predictability of the life he sees on the street. What is lacking and longed for in Víctor's mind is any feeling, any capacity to react in a truly human way to his surroundings. It is clear that Díaz Fernández (like the other authors discussed in this study) sees this dehumanization as a central quality of modern, industrializing Madrid. *La Venus mecánica* and the later essays of Díaz Fernández take great pains to link this dehumanization to the avant-garde aesthetic of the time as well, heralding the new social novel as an important tool to critique inherently urban problems.

Unlike the other novels analyzed in detail here, *La Venus mecánica* does not chronicle a strong differentiation between types of urban space. Those with money and those without, men and women, young and old are all seen spending their leisure time in such places as the Alkázar Theater, the Eslava Dance Hall where Obdulia and Víctor first meet, the Puerta del Sol, the Ritz Hotel, the Hotel Palace and returning to their homes not far from the Gran Vía, which is the geographical center of the novel. The roles of those Madrid citizens in these places of leisure are gendered, however. Almost exclusively, the women are there to sell their services, to contribute their modern notions of beauty to the generation of an entertainment industry. The men are almost all professionals who come as consumers to these spaces. What is more, the female characters have no stable, official income and move often, residing in rented rooms on such streets as the Calle Luchana, Calle del Pez, Calle de Paradiñas and Calle Guzmán el Bueno, most of these found in the working-class Trafalgar and Chamberí neighborhoods just north of the Gran Vía. The male protagonists, on the other hand, all occupy the same residence over the course of the novel. The inhabitants of these two overlapping but gendered worlds meet almost exclusively on the frequently-mentioned Gran Vía, meeting in or outside of places like the Gran Vía Hotel where Víctor lives and the nearby Hotel Suizo where he works, at the Banco de España, at the Madrid-Paris department store, and in the theaters, hotels and cabarets mentioned and located in the maps included here (*Fig. 4.5*).

It is significant that the newly-constructed Gran Vía is the point of union of many different sectors of Madrid's society, the new center of culture, leisure and business (as outlined in Chapter Two), but it also becomes an important and central space for the spectacle of political protest. Seemingly from one moment to the next, the Gran Vía turns from a place of conspicuous consumption and luxury to the location of brutal violence. The outbreak of the 1927 general strike on the Gran Vía is described at one point in the novel from Víctor's point of view. He leans out of the window of the Hotel Gran Vía where he works and, in his words,

la Gran Vía, llena de guardias, tenía ahora fisonomía de campamento.
El sol bruñía las crestas de los edificios, el charol de las cartucheras y el
acero de los fusiles; descendía imperturbable a mezclarse en la retenida
furia de las armas para mostrar una vez más la indiferencia de la Natura-
leza por los angustiosos conflictos de los hombres. (1929: 265)

[The Gran Vía, full of soldiers, now had the appearance of a camp. The
sun burnished the tops of the buildings, the leather of the cartridge belts
and the steel of the rifles; it descended smoothly to mix with the controlled fury of the weapons in order to show once again the indifference
of Nature for the anguished conflicts of men.]

Víctor sees this ferment of political dissent in the safety of his office
above the street, musing on the look of the buildings in the setting
sun and the relationship between Nature and human conflict, search-
ing for an artful way to capture the moment in his next article.
Obdulia, significantly, lives the very same scene first hand, up close.
She witnesses at street level how the aforementioned clash of striking
workers and police on the Gran Vía quickly turns into a full-fledged
battle. When she runs from the Gran Vía to search for safety on the
Calle de Valverde

veía a los huelguistas pasar atropellados, dispersos, perseguidos por las
guardias. Fue en aquel instante cuando un grupo de ellos ganó la calle de
Valverde para escapar de la feroz persecución. Pero allí mismo, frente a
Obdulia, fueron alcanzados por la pareja que les perseguía. Los guardias
descargaron sus sables sobre los hombres que quedaron heridos, pisoteados
por los caballos. Uno, con alpargatas y bufanda verde, tenía la frente rota
de un sablazo. Obdulia, ciega, frenética, erguida como una virgen roja,
increpó a los jinetes desde la acera: –¡Canallas! ¡Canallas! (1929: 272-273).

[she saw the striking protestors go by hurriedly and disperse, chased by
the soldiers. Just then a group of them came down Valverde Street in
order to escape from the ferocious chase. But right there, in front of
Obdulia, they were caught by the pair that was chasing them. The soldiers shot at the men, who were injured and trampled by the horses.
One of them was wearing sandals and a green scarf and his face was torn
open by the blow of a saber. Obdulia, blind, frenetic, straightened up

like a Red Virgin and reprimanded the riders from the sidewalk:
Scoundrels! Scoundrels!]

There is no distant musing or reflection on the visual effects of the sun
for Obdulia. Her active participation in the demonstration is vital to
her development as a character. In important ways, she is more in tune
with what is going on politically than the more intellectual, privileged
Víctor because of her class position. Díaz Fernández describes the experience of being in a stampede of demonstrators being chased by the
police (an experience well-known to the author as he participated in
similar activities in the very same streets he describes). Obdulia cannot
escape being involved in the fray, while Víctor can distance himself at
will. Indeed, his ability to observe from afar helps him to write about it
as a journalist. As has already been mentioned, this objective versus
subjective, intellectual versus first-hand knowledge of the tumultuous
modern experience is one of the central tensions of the novel. The different spatial orientations of these characters are emphasized throughout the novel and are an important part of their very different ways of
reaching political awareness. The underground space of the Modelo
prison cell where the last moments of the novel take place is telling.
Only there, away from the myths of modernity that the novel has
undermined, can the two protagonists find each other and vow to work
together for social change.

By superimposing urban upon literary modes and vice versa, *La
Venus mecánica* is a uniquely perceptive critique of and commentary on
the human side of the age of mass production, in all of its individual and
collective triumphs and trials. Because of persistent attention to the production of urban space, the urbanization of consciousness and the relationship of culture to capital, the novel is urban in the truest sense of the
word. Like the other works examined in this study, it is conscious of its
ideological position in the cultural arena: indeed, this becomes one of
the very themes of the novel itself. Torn between taking pleasure in the
increasingly available mass-produced products and the pain of resulting
alienation, *La Venús mecánica*, like the fictional characters it portrays, is a
sobering voice of dissent in the tumultuous political, social and cultural
environment of Madrid at the end of the Primo de Rivera dictatorship.

CHAPTER V

Madrid Goes to Hollywood: Andrés Carranque de Ríos's *Cinematógrafo*

Augusto M. Torres documents that by 1936 Madrid had a legitimate film industry consisting of 18 film production companies and 90 movie theaters, all of which were created between 1902 and 1936 (1986: 19). There was an established local star system marketing such stars as Imperio Argentina, Rosita Díaz-Gimeno and Pilar Muñoz. The development of this star system was aided by the creation of a wide variety of popular magazines about Spanish film and Spanish film stars such as *¡A Mí ... Películas!, Cine Español, Madrid Cinematográfico, Cinegramas* and *Super-Cine*, just to mention those with the longest print runs. Film had become such an integral part of the lives and imaginations of *madrileños* and had such a dramatic impact on the built environment of the city with the construction of the great movie theaters on the Gran Vía that one cinematic staple of the industry consisted of films that directly referenced the role that the seventh art playedin Madrid's daily life. Light, playful films like *Las entrañas de Madrid* [Madrid from the Inside] (1926), *El pilluelo de Madrid* [Madrid City-Slicker] (1927), *¡Viva Madrid que es mi pueblo!* [Long Live Madrid – My Town!] (1927), *Rosa de Madrid* [The Rose of Madrid] (1928) and the historical *Isidro labrador* [Isidro the Worker] (1923), *Luis Candelas o el bandido de Madrid* [Luis Candelas or the Madrid Bandit] (1926) and *El 2 de Mayo* [The Second of May] (1927) were some of the most popular (1949: Cabero).[1] José Luis Sáenz de Heredia's 1934 comedy *Patricio miró a una estrella* [Patricio Saw a Star] is one such feature-length movie about an ardent filmgoer who falls in love with a movie star and, in order to seduce her, begins to work in a film studio, ultimately becoming a successful actor. A story about the production of the Spanish star system, the film also captured the alienation filmgoers often felt in relation to the events and styles they witnessed on the screen.

Film and the Urbanization of Consciousness

Made quickly with the successful Hollywood formula in mind, these films were at the crossroads of Spanish modernity in that they captured the fears and hopes of urban citizens in the process of negotiating the new spaces of the city and of the movie theater itself.[2] Capturing the immediately recognizable city outside of the doors of the theater, this new medium simultaneously linked Spaniards to some of the increasingly global forms of storytelling made possible by mass production. This new way of capturing and representing modern life through the camera lens was seen as potentially pleasing but also dangerous in that it could possibly be used as a means of surveillance and control. As Walter Benjamin pointed out in his essay "The Work of Art in the Age of Mechanical Reproduction" cited in the previous chapter, film had become the medium of nonauratic art – art finally freed from its earlier religious or cultic function – precisely because it relayed a reorganization of space and time for perception. "The

1. Cabero's 1949 *Historia de la cinematografía española* is the most complete history to date of the Spanish film industry in the first half of the century.
2. The response of popular film was, by and large, one that protected the social status quo. Talens and Zunzunegui (1998) link Spain's film history to the representation of very conservative, Catholic myths and ideologies, as does Gubern in 'El cine y sus mitos' (2000).

equipment-free aspect of reality here has become the height of arti-
fice; the sight of immediate reality has become an orchid in the land
of technology" (1968: 232). Film expresses in a unique way the desire
to, as Benjamin put it, "bring things closer spatially and humanly,"
meaning that it grows out of an urge to "get hold of an object at very
close range by way of its likeness, its reproductions" (1968: 245).
This sense of closeness and intimacy associated with film is a para-
dox, of course, because film is the product of a market-driven industry that profits from people's feelings of alienation.[3]

The 1936 novel *Cinematógrafo*, with its cinematographic narrative style and its ironic, often humorous depiction of the fledgling
Spanish film industry of the 1920s and '30s in Madrid, is the narrative counterpart to these self-reflexive films.[4] The fate of the novel as
a work of literature is emblematic of what has happened to much
prose written in the earlier decades of the twentieth century in Spain.[5]
Contemporary Spanish literary criticism has never been able to find

---

3. See Larson (2007) on the commonalities between the cinematic philosophies of
   Spanish avant-garde filmmaker Sobrevila and Benjamin.
4. Morris looks at the lasting effects that popular film had on Spanish poets such
   as Rafael Alberti, Luis Cernuda and Federico García Lorca and the novelists
   Benjamín Jarnés, José Díaz Fernández, Francisco Ayala and Rosa Chacel.
5. At first glance it seems incomprehensible that *Cinematógrafo* could have been
   selected by Entrambasaguas in 1968 to be included in a series on the best Spanish
   novels of the century. The other novels included in this ninth volume are Félix
   Urabayen's *Don Amor Volvió a Toledo*, Ramón Ledesma Miranda's *Almudena, o historia de viejos personajes*, Samuel Ros's *Los vivos y los muertos* and Agustín de Foxá's
   Madrid de Corte a Cheka, all of them sharing decidedly conservative, Catholic
   values and this last considered a prime example of Fascist literature. Its inclusion
   can only be explained by the strange fact that Entrambasaguas apologizes repeatedly for the youthful excesses of Carranque de Ríos, reminding the reader that the
   author critiques all governments and revolutionary groups. Only by apologizing
   for Carranque's political involvement can Entrambasaguas include the work of a
   young man who, because of his death right before the outbreak of the Civil War
   in 1936, ironically could be seen as being politically neutral in Spain in 1968.

room in its rigid social/avant-garde dichotomy for novels that draw on both aesthetics. Like Carmen de Burgos and José Díaz Fernández, Carranque de Ríos used modernist and avant-garde techniques to further enhance the impact of the social themes of his novels. He belongs to the movement described by Díaz Fernández as "el nuevo romanticismo," which found a middle ground between the avant-garde and the social. In Díaz Fernández's defense of Ortega y Gasset in *El nuevo romanticismo* he says:

> Defender una estética puramente formal, donde la palabra pierda todos aquellos valores que no sean musicales o plásticos, es un fiasco intelectual, un fraude que se hace a la época en que vivimos que es de las más ricas en conflictos y problemas. Cuando Ortega y Gasset habla de la deshumanización del arte no lo propugna. Pero unos cuantos han tomado el rábano por las hojas y han empezado a imitar en España lo que ya en el mundo estaba en trance de desaparecer. (1930: 69)

> [To defend a purely formal aesthetic, where the word loses all of the values that are not musical or plastic, is an intellectual fiasco, a fraud that makes the age in which we live rich in conflicts and problems. When Ortega y Gasset talks about the dehumanization of art he doesn't defend it. But some people have thrown the baby out with the bath water and have begun to imitate in Spain what in the rest of Europe was about to disappear.]

Although he uses the term avant-garde throughout his essay, Díaz Fernández calls for a broadly modernist aesthetic that is more rooted in and able to comment on the reality of early twentieth-century Spain. He ascribes to the theory still popular today that Spain lags behind the rest of Europe, but the author stresses that this does not necessarily need to be the case: that through a more socially-aware and critical form of the avant-garde, the artist can reflect on the experience of modernity in significant and important ways.

In *Cinematógrafo*, his third novel, Carranque de Ríos consciously sought to appeal to a wide reading public. Fulgencio Castañar offers no concrete figures but groups it with other popular, social novels that sold well.[6] The author's first novel was undoubtedly helped along by its prologue by Pío Baroja. Carranque de Ríos met Baroja while he was working as an unpaid actor on the set of the first film version of *Zalacaín el aventurero* in 1927. All of Carranque de Ríos's three full-length novels (*Uno*, 1934; *La vida difícil*, 1935; *Cinematógrafo*, 1936) are similar to the urban novels of Pío Baroja in their realism and narrative recreation of easily recognizable characters with problems specific to Madrid. They were more overtly political than the avant-garde narratives of Carranque de Ríos's contemporaries such as Benjamín Jarnés, Rosa Chacel, Corpus Barga, Pedro Salinas and José Martínez Ruiz, however.

In his prologue to the 1997 edition of *Cinematógrafo*, Antonio Muñoz Molina admits that "nuestra cultura es tan incompleta, tan azarosa, que yo no lo habría leído si no me hubiesen encargado este prólogo" [our culture is so incomplete, so capricious, that I never would have read this book if I hadn't been asked to write the prologue] (1997: 17). *Cinematógrafo*, its protagonist Álvaro Jiménez, and indeed the life of Carranque de Ríos himself are all perfect vehicles through which to see and understand the nature of Madrid's modern experience at the beginning of the twentieth century. Carranque de Ríos (1902-1936) is one of the most organic of Spanish intellectuals in the Gramscian sense of the word. He was born into a poor family and raised in the La Latina neighborhood of Madrid. A man of contradictions, he received an incomplete grade school education yet was comfortable in (though not uncritical of) Madrid's intellectual café society. He supported himself by working on and off as a day laborer doing construction and as a journalist (Fortea 1972: 23-41).[7] The same man who at a young age was put in jail for starting

---

6. For information on novels and the Spanish cultural marketplace between 1898 and 1936, see Castañar and Fernández Cifuentes.
7. Fortea's biography of Carranque de Ríos includes chapters on his family, work history, military service, jail time, travel and informal education. There is little mention of his literary techniques, styles, or influences other than those of Pío

an anarchist labor organization (naming it Spartacus, no less) also devoted himself wholeheartedly to making a reputation in the Spanish film industry which was producing decidedly apolitical, popular, sentimental films that upheld very traditional values (Pérez Rojas 1986: 59-63). Carranque de Ríos, an undeniably dashing young fellow in the Errol Flynn mold, (*Fig. 5.1*) had small acting roles in five movies (4 silent, 1 sound) made in Spain.[8] Most are of poor quality, made with low budgets using formulaic scripts under just the kind of conditions described in *Cinematógrafo*.

After being released from jail in 1931, Carranque de Ríos spent some time in the South of France and Paris, unsuccessfully looking for work but finding time to write. In Paris he befriended the surrealist writer René Crevel. After spending some months in Barcelona in 1933, involved with his anarchist friends in planning demonstrations and strikes, Carranque de Ríos returned to Madrid and began to write in earnest. It is at this point that his articles start to appear regularly in important newspapers. *Uno* was published by Espasa-Calpe in 1934 and was well received by critics in newspapers such as *Crónica*, *Heraldo de Madrid* and *Índice Literario*, according to Fortea (1972: 63). Carranque de Ríos had made such a name for himself by 1935 that he was invited to participate in the International Conference in Defense of Culture, Henri Barbusse's effort at uniting intellectuals capable of speaking out against the conservative nationalist movements emerging across Europe. Carranque de Ríos was in good company. The list of foreign guests included Gorki, Brecht, Pasternack, Dos Passos, Forster and Neruda. From France, Gide, Malraux, Bloch and Cassou attended. Valle-Inclán, Manuel Azaña, Antonio Machado, Juan Ramón Jiménez, García Lorca, Sender and others traveled from Spain to participate. Carranque de Ríos reported to the *Heraldo*

Baroja and Nietzsche. Fortea compiled a collection of Carranque de Ríos's complete works in 1998.

8.   Carranque de Ríos's *Al Hollywood madrileño* (1927), *La del soto del parral* (1928), *El héroe de Cascorro* (1929), *Zalacaín el aventurero* (1929), and *Miguelón, el último contrabandista* (1933) (Cinemedia CD-ROM, 1996).

de Madrid on the events of the conference. On the day before he went to Paris, Carranque de Ríos wrote the following:

> El Congreso comienza el día 21 y sus tareas creo que durarán unos quince días. En ese tiempo se examinará la labor literaria realizada por los diversos países, las trabas que por parte del nazismo se pone a determinados escritores y las persecuciones de que éstos son objeto por Gobiernos de una y otra tendencia. Los acuerdos han de ser muy importantes, y, sobre todo, adquieren importancia al estar avalados por las firmas de lo más destacado de la intelectualidad mundial. (cited in Fortea 1972: 68)

> [The Congress begins on the 21st and its work will take place over a period of fifteen says. In that time we will examine the literature produced in various countries, the obstacles that Nazism is putting in the way of certain authors and the persecution of certain authors that is taking place by a number of different types of governments. The agreements will most likely be very important and, most of all, will acquire even greater importance when they are sealed with the signatures of the most select of world intellectuals.]

Carranque de Ríos, always short on funds, was to stay with his good friend Crevel in Paris for the duration of the conference. His plan went awry when Crevel committed suicide the day before his arrival.

Madrid's Unique Film History

The semi-autobiographical *Cinematógrafo* follows the adventures and trials of a young man named Álvaro Giménez who cannot identify with any one group yet whose individual actions are revolutionary. Most of the novel is devoted to the intertwined stories of the lives of a group of people involved in Madrid's fledgling film industry in the 1930s, although one brief section (part of Álvaro's first-person manuscript) is devoted to the misadventures of the protagonist in the small town of Damiel, where he goes to rest from the trials and deprivations of the city. *Cinematógrafo* begins with a short section called "Otras noticias" [Other News] which sets the tone for the entire novel. "Por ahora todo lo que se refiera a la vida de Pablo Gómez quedará reducido en *Cinematógrafo* a esta especie de nota póstuma: 'Pablo Gómez no fue otra cosa que un vulgar prestidigitador,'" (1997: 25) [For now everything that has to do with the life of Pablo Gómez will be reduced in *Cinematógrafo* to this type of posthumous note: 'Pablo Gómez was nothing but a crude slight-of-hand trickster], reads the very first sentence of the novel. Purposefully disorienting, this entrance into the novel is self-reflexive and refers to the art of deception inherent in all storytelling, simultaneously exemplifying all of the ways the fictional characters are about to fool, lie and cheat one another. The profession of Pablo Gómez

> consistía en hacer bailar a unas gallinas encima de una plataforma de acero... Las gallinas, a una orden de Pablo Gómez, comenzaban a agitarse para bailar durante unos minutos. Solamente Pablo Gómez tenía conocimiento de que las gallinas danzaban encima de una plataforma calentada por la electricidad. (1997: 26)

> [consisted of making some chickens dance on top of a steel platform... The chickens, acting on Pablo Gómez's orders, would shake and dance for a few minutes. Only Pablo Gómez knew that the chickens were dancing on a heated and electrified surface.]

Of course, times are difficult and soon Pablo Gómez is hungry and has no way of providing for himself.

> El artista se encontró sin público. El drama fue desarrollándose en un período de días. Un drama silencioso y falto de belleza. Pablo Gómez empezó por la gallina más vieja: una gallina que ya no podía danzar sobre la plancha caliente. Los demás animales fueron devorados más tarde, hasta no quedar una sola gallina en posición de actuar sobre el infierno de la plataforma. (1997: 26)

> [The artist found himself with no audience. This drama came about over the period of a few days. A silent drama lacking any and all beauty. Pablo Gómez began with the oldest chicken: a chicken who couldn't dance

on the hot grill any more. The other animals were devoured later, until
there was not a single chicken left to perform on the hellish platform.]

The humorous but pathetic image of the tortured dancing chickens
promptly overlays the following section when the actors/students of
Academia Film are treated in a similar fashion by the Sancho brothers. Made to perform out of desperation and hunger, they make
wretched films full of impossible, fantastically escapist plots that in
no way reflect the situation in which they work and live. Tony, the
young son of Doña Luisa, for example, is full of hope that he will be
the next Charlie Chaplin. Mother and son scrape together enough
money to pay for the exploitative "acting lessons" at Academia Film,
but Tony dies from malnutrition and lack of medical care. Those who
produce culture in Madrid at this time are not portrayed as mere
tyrants, however. They are simply caught in the same trap with everyone else, existing in an environment where the credo is "survival of the
fittest." Pablo Gómez appears only briefly in the beginning of novel,
never to be heard from again until someone in passing refers to him
as "el artista desaparecido Pablo Gómez. En la reunión se habla de él
como de algo extraordinario y difícil de imitar. Llegó a deber ochenta
y tres cafés, sin contar quince pesetas que le fueron prestadas por el
camarero" (1997: 91) [the disappeared artist Pablo Gómez. At meetings they talk about him as someone extraordinarily hard to imitate.
He was in debt for the equivalent of up to eighty-three coffees, not
counting the fifteen pesetas the waiter lent to him.]

From the beginning of the novel, therefore, the relationship between
art and capital is harshly criticized. Artists and the only people with the
time and skills to be creative–writers, journalists, filmmakers—have to
engage in the most cynical forms of exploitation and deception. Pablo
Gómez is one fictional character granted the dignity of a name, but the
novel is full of many anonymous characters who appear and then disap-
pear in a fluid, turbulent stream of *madrileños* alternately enamored of
and disappointed by what the modern city has to offer. Towards the
beginning of the novel, when the protagonist Álvaro still clings to his
hope of becoming a journalist, he goes to an editor and proposes two
stories: "Como viven los que no pueden vivir," [How those who can't

survive live] about the families that live under the bridges of the Manzanares River, and "Madrid y sus minas de carbón," [Madrid and its
coal mines] about the women and children who rely solely on what
the coal trucks drop in the street for their survival. The editor rejects the
stories as "mera literatura," (1997: 215) [mere literature] suggesting that
Álvaro should write stories like other successful journalists, some of
the best of which include titles such as "Hablando con el hombre más
gordo de Cuenca" [Talking to the fattest man in Cuenca], "Cómo se
crían las uvas moscatel" [How moscatel grapes are grown] and "Un
limpiabotas que hace comedias" [A shoeshine who writes plays] (1997:
216). Having fled the closed, oppressive environment of the small
town of Damiel after compromising the upstanding reputations of his
friend Juan and his mother by insisting on visiting the Casa del Pueblo,
Álvaro finds himself without any money, and decides to make it back to
Madrid on foot, over a period of a few days. His shoes cause blisters on
his feet the first day, but no matter, because someone promptly steals
them. He enters the small town of Manzanares and, hungry and cold,
begs the President of the Casino to allow him to read some poetry aloud
during a large gathering of the town. The president is kind-hearted, so
he asks him if he can give a speech on literature for the townspeople.

> Álvaro pensó en el libro que guardaba en un bolsillo de su americana
> y se le ocurrió mostrárselo al presidente.
> —¿Y no sería igual el que leyera algunas poesías de este libro?
> —Bien, lea estas poesías, pero indique que los versos están escritos
> por usted.
> —Comprenda que eso es imposible—añadió para el presidente—.
> Pueden darse cuenta del engaño.
> —Entonces no digan nada. Usted lee unas cuantas poesías sin decir
> quién es el autor. De esta manera creerán que los versos han sido escritos
> por usted. (1997: 288)

> [Álvaro thought about the book that he had in the pocket of his
> jacket and it occurred to him to show it to the president.
> —What do you think of me reading some poems from this book?
> —Fine, read those poems, but make people think that you wrote
> them.

—You have to understand that that is impossible – he responded —.
They might figure out that it's a lie.
—Then don't say anything. Read some poems without saying who
the author is. That way they'll think that you wrote the poems.]

The author of the book is Antonio Machado, one of Álvaro's favorite
poets. The crowd is completely uninterested in the poetry that Álvaro
pretends is his own. His woeful performance is underscored by his
shame at being in the situation in the first place. He apologetically
takes the stage, saying "Señoras y señores –ya he dicho cuál era mi
propósito... Yo no quiero molestarles lo más mínimo... Terminaré en
seguida... Solamente necesito que me concedan diez minutos. En
diez minutos habré terminado" [Ladies and gentlemen – I've already
told you why I'm here... I don't want to bother you at all... I'll be
done soon... I only need ten minutes of your time. I'll be done in ten
minutes] (1997: 295-296). After the poems are read, "Álvaro hizo
pausa, pero no escuchó ningún aplauso. En cambio, se oyó reír por
donde estaba el secretario. Dándose cuenta de la escena, el presidente
rompió a aplaudir. También aplaudieron los músicos, aunque estos
contados aplausos no hacían sino destacar la risa que se extendían en
algunos corros. Alguien pidió que cesaran las burlas" [Álvaro paused,
but he didn't hear any applause. Instead, he heard someone near the
secretary laughing. Realizing what was happening, the president
began to clap. The musicians clapped too, although that only made
the laughter coming from the back more obvious. Someone asked for
the teasing to stop]. Álvaro's performance ends abruptly when "se
escuchó una voz que decía: '¡Queremos bailar! ¿Por qué no toca la
música?'" [a voice called out 'We want to dance! Why isn't the music
playing?'] (1997: 297). Álvaro collects only enough money to buy a
couple of meals. He manages to leave the town well-fed and rested
only because the caretaker of the Casino has appreciated his recital of
Machado and takes pity on him. This segment is only one in a series
of similar humiliations that eventually lead to the protagonist's
demise.

There is only one artist in the novel who is admired by Álvaro and
able to survive in the city, a nameless photographer in the Plaza de

España. One morning in particular Álvaro is hungry and only has enough money to buy a slice of bread from a bakery where an unusually pretty young woman works. He buys the bread but cannot eat it because he is ashamed that the woman will witness him hungrily devour the pitifully small meal and he gives it to the birds. Álvaro is impressed by the photographer, who is sitting on a bench next to his tripod, happily eating his simple but bountiful lunch from an aluminum container.

> Enfrente de mí el fotógrafo sigue dándole a las mandíbulas. En los lados de su modesto aparato de retratar hay muchas fotografías. Estos postales son la garantía de que allí se trabajaba como es debido. Él es un pobre retratista que no tiene nada que ver con esos capitanes de industria que poseen a la puerta de su casa una serie de premios y medallas ... que saben reventar una huelga para después rebajar los jornales, pero que ignora 'quién es Luisito'. Esto es lo que él no sabe, lo que él no conocerá nunca.... (1997: 219)

> [In front of me the photographer keeps his jaws working away. On all sides of his humble image-capturing device there are many photographs. Those cards are proof that he has real honest-to-goodness work. He is a humble portrait artist who doesn't have anything to do with those captains of industry who show off at their doors their series of prizes and medals ... who know how to quell a strike only to later tone down the newspapers, but who don't know anything about the common man. This is what he doesn't know, what he will never know ....]

Álvaro can only dream of being employed in such a way as to practice his skills and not go hungry. The photographer owns his modest equipment and thus is free to work as much as he requires and on his own terms. This is what the motivated, creative Álvaro searches for throughout the novel and, tragically, never finds.

In *Cinematógrafo* the offices of the film company "Academia Films" are located in a place that is of great importance in Spanish film history: on Bravo Murillo, the street where the first Lumière brothers' short films were seen by the Spanish royal family in 1898. This chronotope makes a spatial connection that forces the reader to make the temporal comparison between 1898 and 1930s Madrid. Combined, they draw attention to the stark contrast between film's introduction to the Spanish elite and the difficulties that the Spanish film industry underwent in the 1920s and 1930s. How the director and producer, the Sancho brothers, and their rival, Señor Rocamora of "Rocamora Films" make movies is one of the main concerns of the novel. It narrates the lives of the students at "Academia Film," a ragged, underfed lot obsessed with images from the silver screen and film magazines with pictures of movie stars accompanying articles on their fabulous lives. They are described as

> … ellos, soñadores de un arte nuevo—un arte que nacía en España con un aire mediocre. Se comía poco, pero se soñaba con la niebla blanca que se aplasta sobre las pantallas del mundo. Al fin y al cabo, lo único agradable de la vida es lo que pasa por nuestro lado como un sueño. Y esto era ya bastante para aquellos hombres que aguardaban a poder viajar en primera clase, a vivir en buenos hoteles y a celebrar interviús con los redactores de las publicaciones cinematográficas. (1997: 27)

> [dreamers of a new art – an art that was born in Spain in a mediocre way. They ate very little, but they dreamed about the white mist that distorts the screens of the world. In the end, the only enjoyable thing about life is what happens, dream-like, at our side. And that was enough for those men who hoped to be able to travel in first class, to live in good hotels and conduct interviews with the editors of the film publications.]

The students barely manage to pay for screen tests and classes at the film academy, the outtakes of which are edited in such a way as to become the actual films the Sancho brothers show in theaters. That is, if film is rolling in the camera at all. Often, they make the student actors think they are being filmed just to encourage them and to make sure they come back to be exploited on a long-term basis. The Sancho brothers justify these working conditions by telling the actors that "esto del cine es muy verde. Todos tenemos que ayudar a la industria cinematográfica y ustedes son los primeros que tienen que cumplir ese deber" (1997: 85) [this film business is very new. We must all help the film industry along and you are the first ones who have to complete this duty]. In another speech given by the Sancho brothers, José authoritatively tells the students:

[e]s conveniente que ustedes no olvidan nunca que el cine es un arte de sombras–este último pertenecía a una revista profesional–. Un arte…; en fin, ustedes me entienden perfectamente. Creo que en Norteamérica andan tras de inventar la película parlante. Dudo que esto llegue a ser una realidad. El cine es y debe de ser un 'arte de sombras'. Por tanto, acostúmbrense ustedes a no exagerar los movimientos y a no hacer los gestos demasiados expresivos. Si el cine es un 'arte de sombras…' (1997: 53).

[you should never forget that film is an art of shadows—this last statement came right from a professional magazine –. An art …; well, you understand me perfectly. I think that in North America they're trying to invent a talking movie. I doubt that this will ever happen. Film is and should be 'an art of shadows.' So, get used to not making any exaggerated movements and don't make your faces too expressive. Because film is 'an art of shadows…']

An art of shadows, indeed, in which the participants are deceived and the truth behind the making of the films is well-hidden. Since the film industry in Madrid (and film in general) is so closely tied to capital and the economic system is precarious, those involved at this time in making movies for the Spanish film market were amateurs who relied heavily on foreign manuals and film magazines which always made filmmaking seem easier than it actually was (de Diego 1986: 155-159).

The Sancho brothers live off the dreams of their tuition-paying acting students until the day they receive funding from Señor Poch, a Catalan living in Madrid after having made a fortune from his coffee plantations in Ecuador. Encouraged by a con-man named Norberto Robledal from the United States, Poch and the Sancho brothers decide to make a movie about love lost and found in Galicia because they want to capture the overseas market.[9] They work under the mis-

---

9. The character Norberto Robledal is based on Spanish film director Benito Perojo. Perojo worked in major film studios in Paris, Berlin and Hollywood making

guided notion that every Galician in North and South America will
want to see their film. Robledal has lied to them about the money-
making possibilities of this Galician love story. Out of spite he
deceives the film producer and director by encouraging them to make
a film that is obsolete even before it is completed, because by the time
they finish only sound films will be marketable and therefore their
investment will have been a waste. The Sancho brothers make the
film, though, with very little money. Curiously, it ends up being
nothing more than a long commercial for Poch's coffee, a perfect
example of the film industry's first product placement techniques.
Tied to the production of a film is the investment of capital which
can't help but control the nature of the final product. This is exempli-
fied in the text of the screenplay *El que no corre, vuela* embedded in
the novel, written by a character who is a hack writer named Joaquín
Nuño for Señor Poch and the Sancho brothers.

> 'Por distintas calles de Madrid se ven grupos de transeúntes que van
> corriendo en varias direcciones. Entre los que corren hay niños, viejos,
> mujeres, soldados, etc. Un chófer abandona su taxi y se une a los que
> pasan.... Un ciego que está pidiendo limosna abandona al perro que le
> sirve de lazarillo, abre los ojos, demostrando que su ceguera es completa-
> mente fingida, y se coge del brazo del primero que pasa. A la puerta de
> una iglesia está un cojo. Tira la muleta y desaparece tras los que corren.
> Como obedeciendo a un señal, se paran enfrente de un café. En una de
> las mesas se halla un caballero gordo y optimista. Cuando la gente se
> coloca alrededor de la mesa, el caballero coge una taza y se la lleva a los
> labios con intención de beber. Al estar la taza en alto se acercará la
> máquina tomavistas hasta que se lea perfectamente ¡Tomad cafés Ecua-
> dor! Todo el público mirará con envidia al caballero gordo. Éste, lleno de

---

Spanish versions of German, French and American films. Gubern says that '[n]o
fue, ciertamente, un director original, pero aspiraba a crear un cine situado a la
altura de la burguesía urbana, como el que dominaba en la producción contemporánea de París o Hollywood' [He certainly was not an original director, but his
aspiration was to create movies for the urban middle class, like the film that domi-
nated production in Paris and Hollywood] (2000: 121).

satisfacción, sorberá el café despacio dando a entender que está bebiendo
un licor exquisito.' (1997: 176)

[‘Through several different Madrid streets are seen groups of passersby running in different directions. Among them are children, old folks,
women, soldiers, etc. A chauffeur gets out of his taxi and joins those
walking…. A blind man begging leaves the dog that was serving as his
guide, he opens his eyes, revealing that his blindness was a sham, and he
takes the arm of the first person who passes by. In the doorway of a
church there's a crippled man. He throws away his crutch and disappears
behind the runners. As if obeying a signal, they stop in front of a café. At
one of the tables is a fat and very upbeat man. When all of the people
gather around the table, the man picks up a cup and brings it to his lips
as if he were going to drink. When the cup is raised the camera
approaches until you read, Drink Ecuador Coffee! The audience will
look enviously at the fat gentleman. Full of satisfaction, he will drink the
coffee slowly as if he were drinking an exquisite liquid.']

Cinematógrafo expresses disillusionment that something as entertain-
ing and potentially magical as a film becomes mired down in the
details of greed and exploitation. When the films made by the Sancho brothers are finally released, they are shown for a short period of
time. The filmmakers don't despair over this, however, because it
takes just a couple of weeks to piece another one together and the
process starts all over again, as long as someone with a camera or a
product to advertise is making a small profit.

Cinematógrafo demonstrates how urban development in Madrid
at the beginning of the twentieth century parallels the Spanish film
industry. Both are image-obsessed, striving to emulate modern cities
like New York, London and Paris, but through the lens of Hollywood. The forms they both ultimately take are not the result of any
rational, carefully-considered long-term plan but are shown to be
subject to the whims of capital. On one hand Spanish films are participating fully in a booming industry, being shown in the beautiful,
modern art deco theaters of the Gran Vía like the Callao and Capitol
and advertised in popular photo magazines. The reality of how they
were made, however, and then received by a Spanish public that by

and large ignored them in favor of American and bigger-budget European movies, shows how Spaniards as cultural producers and consumers did not always discover or define their own experience of modern life. Just as Señor Poch uses film solely as a means to advertise his Café Ecuador, large national and international companies such as Camel, Phillips and Coca-Cola used the ultra-modern Edificio Capitol to advertise their products. The novel describes how those with the power to construct their urban environment for the good of its inhabitants failed to do so because they looked to other models for inspiration, models which themselves were based largely on a glamorized façade.

Visualizing Spatial Boundaries in *Cinematógrafo*

There is a strong sense of place that is inextricably and directly linked to the urbanization of consciousness throughout *Cinematógrafo*. Madrid's inhabitants eat in cafés in the Puerta del Sol, Doña Luisa and Tony live on the Calle Toledo off of the Plaza Mayor, Álvaro lives in the La Latina neighborhood, various characters stroll and work along Atocha, Cuatro Caminos, the Plaza de España and the Gran Vía, and other roads in the center of Madrid. Their comings and goings are described in great detail. On the surface modern Madrid would seem to provide many opportunities for its inhabitants to come and go freely and quickly, but the fictional characters in *Cinematógrafo*, in spite of their constant walking and riding on the metro and *tranvías,* are trapped in their own particular spaces and endanger themselves when they try to break free. For example, when Álvaro and two friends enjoy the rare pleasure of driving around Madrid in an old moving truck they decide to explore parts of the city they don't usually visit. They drive from the Paseo del Prado past the Plaza Colón and start down the Castellana until they are singled out when they are stopped and told by an angry policeman that their "lata de sardinas" [sardine can] (1997: 227), unlike all of the other more expensive vehicles on the road, is not allowed to be seen in such an important, glamorous part of town. Álvaro directly participates in the northern urban expansion discussed in Chapter Two of this book when he suffers a brief stint as a construction worker building upscale housing along the outskirts of the Princesa, traveling relatively far where there is as yet no transportation, the work ravaging his delicate writer's hands.

Another clear instance of the politicization of represented space occurs when Tony, whose mother strictly forbids him from stepping foot beyond the Calle de Toledo without her, catches a fatal illness (left unnamed but presumably a typhoid-like sickness) when he sneaks his way out of the house one afternoon. He is often depicted in the novel staring off towards the San Isidro cemetery and an open space called the Pradera. He finally gets to see this area up close when he makes his way east down the Calle de Toledo to the Puerta de Toledo, past the Glorieta de las Pirámides, through a train tunnel, thrilled to "conocer aquellos lugares que ahora se mostraban de forma tan distinta a cuando él los miraba desde la ventanilla de su buhardilla" [get to know those places that now seemed so different than when he saw them from the small window of his attic home] (1997: 197). At the edge of the Manzanares right at the Paseo de los Pontones, Tony bathes in the Manzanares River, whose water "bajaba con poca corriente y mostraba una gran suciedad" [barely trickled down and seemed absolutely filthy] (1997: 200). Oblivious to the dangers of the water where he sees homeless families bathing, the innocent Tony catches his death in the place of his daydreams, trying to fulfill his child's fantasy of independence and adventure. Tony finally experiences, or makes real for himself, the places he had previously only seen from afar.

When a diagram of the geographic locations mentioned in the novel is superimposed on a map of Madrid, we can recognize two significant patterns: 1) three circular zones (*Fig 5.2*); and 2) a strong centripetal force (*Fig. 5.3*). When all of the events of the novel are mapped, the central zone is the most dense. It is where the majority of the novel takes place and where the narrators engage in their daily activities. The second, larger zone includes still-familiar spaces, but spaces where the more sporadic and simultaneously more significant events of the characters' lives (and deaths) take place. The third zone is where the most exceptional activities take place, where the characters go to try to realize their dreams and to imagine a better future for themselves.

"En Madrid el hombre es una mala bestia. ¡Una bestia hambrienta que a veces no puede ni mudarse de camisa!" [In Madrid men live like condemned beasts. Hungry beasts who sometimes can't even change their shirts!] (1997: 236). This frustration that Felipe expresses during his brief trip to the country permeates the entire novel and is felt as a strong centripetal force that makes a prison of the central area where the main characters live and spend most of their time. Luisa, Tony, Felipe and Álvaro all live in the first zone – the central zone of the novel formed by three points: the Calle Cava Baja, the Calle de Toledo, and La Latina. The boundaries of the larger, second zone rest on three points: to the west the aqueduct in the Calle de Bailén and the Calle de Segovia where Álvaro commits suicide, to the south the Manzanares River at the end of the Paseo de los Pontones where Tony contracts his fatal fever, to the east the City Morgue at the foot of the Calle Isabel, where Felipe is called to identify Álvaro's body, and the Calle de la Cruz off of the Puerta del Sol where Felipe learns that his love for Luisa will be unrequited. The third and largest zone has an overall northern shift, with the boundaries lying on the Calle Bravo Murillo, the Avenida de la Princesa, and the location of the National Library.

All of the main characters regularly walk a long distance out of the main living area of Zone 1 to fulfill their dreams and/or to improve their employment status. This desire to get out of their current situation consistently pushes the characters in a northerly direction. Luisa buys her everyday purchases very close to her home, on the Plaza de la Cebada, but travels a bit further for her shoes to the Calle Preciados. On a similar scale, Álvaro and Felipe often meet for drinks at various locations in the central area, but when Felipe finally gets the opportunity to take Luisa out for a special night, the couple travels a bit further, walking to a café on the Calle de la Cruz close to the Puerta del Sol – further from home, but remaining inside Zone Two.

Álvaro is initially pulled out of these two zones and into Zone Three, into the rapidly-gentrifying renovations of the Calle Princesa

in the hope of earning a living as a construction worker. After only
one day he returns, stops briefly at a medical clinic on the Calle Legan-
itos where he receives cursory medical care, then returns home to walk
the streets of La Latina until he can settle on another way to make a
living. All of the main characters meet and travel over a period of a
few months back and forth to the Rocamora film studio, which is
located north of the Quevedo metro station, on Bravo Murillo. When
Álvaro and his friends drive down Recoletos towards the northwest in
a borrowed moving truck to discover for themselves the urban expansion that they have been hearing about, they are deterred by a policeman from going any further than the Plaza Colón. Álvaro's one and
only trip to the Biblioteca Nacional where he consults a dictionary for
the first time (looking up the word "anarchist" to see if he fits the
description of the archetype that his friends use to describe him) ends
when the scholars working there make him feel unwelcome. There is
an obvious northern/southern line across which the working-class
characters are not allowed to go without being deterred. The northern
region of the city is an area that promises the fulfillment of the dreams
of the main characters, but they are directly and indirectly expelled
from these more open, developing neighborhoods. Urban planning
histories of the 1920s and 1930s show, as we saw in Chapter Two, that
the northern extension of the Castellana was reserved for the institutions of economic, academic and political power. The impact of urban
planning can plainly be seen in the relative locations of the prominent
geographical points of the novel as understood against the history of
the city: a chronotope on a grand scale.

  Cinematógrafo uncovers a geography of social crisis that is directly
related to the ways that urban space was being destroyed and created
during the first third of the twentieth century. Also of interest in the
novel is the great variety of narrative techniques used to communicate this crisis. Carranque de Ríos resorts to several avant-garde,
experimental narrative techniques in order to communicate the
chaotic, disjointed nature of life in Madrid in the 1930s, to great
effect. Not surprisingly, the novel has the structure and feel of a film.

The author often employs an original technique whereby the longer blocks of uninterrupted text narrated in the third person are broken up by short, cumulative sentences in quotations which simulate the now-lost narrative technique of the intertitles used in silent films. One example:

> Los caballeros entraron en el cementerio a continuación de los hombres que llevaban el ataúd. No atreviéndose a hacer lo mismo, Tony curioseó asomando a la puerta. Contempló lápidas y cruces de piedra. En la mayoría de las tumbas se veían ramos de flores. 'Entonces recordó que había hecho muy mal en cortar una rosa de uno de los tiestos de doña Luisa.' (1997: 198)

> [The gentlemen entered the cemetery followed by the men who carried the coffin. Not daring to do the same, Tony's curiosity was increased by snooping around the door. He looked at tombstones and stone crosses. On most of the tombs lay bunches of flowers. 'Then he realized that he had done something wrong by cutting one of the roses off Luisa's vines.']

After this sentence, the narration continues as before to tell of Tony's first adventure outside of his neighborhood. There is no other reason for this last sentence to be in quotation marks other than to separate it, almost imposing it on the third-person narration as if from outside. This is just one of many instances where the reader is made aware of the hands of the authors and narrators.

Cinematógrafo is divided into four parts or "Scenes" ("Primera," "Segunda," "Tercera" and "Cuarta") separated by brief examples of the kind of snippets of gossip found in popular film magazines. These initially appear nonsensical but upon closer inspection announce the tone of each section, often relying on an ironic contrast between the idealized lives of celebrities and the miserable struggle for survival by the fictional characters living in Madrid. The first fragment states simply, "Peter Lynne debe su fama de actor cimematográfico a su manera de fumar en pipa. Gracias a esta cualidad fue visto en un café por mister Barry y contratado en el acto para trabajar en la película *Marineros alegres*. Después de este film, Peter Lynne no ha conocido más que éxito tras éxito" [Peter Lynne owes his fame as a film actor to the way he smokes his pipe. Thanks to this mannerism of his he was spotted in a café by Mr. Barry and hired on the spot to work on the film *Happy Sailors*. After this film, Peter Lynne has known nothing but success upon success] (1997: 36). The ease with which one (with a little elegance and some luck) can become a film star contrasts sharply with the bitterly disappointing experiences of the students of Academia Film, who nevertheless seem to hang on to any shred of hope, encouraged by these very same types of misinformation. The next "Scene" is preceded by this brief bit of information: "Nació en Dakota del Sur (EE.UU.) un 14 de mayo. Estatura: cinco pies y cuatro pulgadas y media. Pasatiempos favoritos: el tenis y la natación" [Born in South Dakota (U.S.A.) on the 14th of May. Height: five feet, four and a half inches. Favorite pastimes: tennis and swimming] (1997: 95). The second "Scene" introduces us to the young protagonist Álvaro and his challenges working for a sensationalistic newspaper in the morning and digging holes for the foundations of high-priced housing along the Princesa in the afternoons. His muscles are throbbing with pain and his hands are damaged by blisters not from swimming and tennis but from back-breaking work under difficult conditions. The third "Scene" is just as deceivingly innocent: "En cuanto a las corbatas de Lewis Rudolph, es ya del dominio público que son las más famosas y las más apreciadas por los elegantes. Solamente en la película *Días de gran lujo*, Lewis Rudolph exhibe cerca de dos docenas. Digamos también que el gris es el color favorito de Lewis Rudolph" [When it comes to Lewis Rudolph's ties, it is well-known to the public that they are the most famous and elegant of all. In *Days of Great Luxury* alone, Lewis Rudolph wears almost two dozen of them. We will say, too, that gray is Lewis Rudolph's favorite color] (1997: 157). The third "Scene" focuses primarily on the battle against hunger and victimization undertaken by many *madrileños* during the 1920s and 1930s. The fourth and last of these dividing fragments reads:

> guardias de pie, guardias de a caballo y agentes de policía secreta vigilaban todo el trayecto por donde tenía que pasar la fúnebre comitiva. Los

hombres se descubrían respetuosamente mientras las mujeres, con los ojos cargados de lágrimas, arrojaban ramos de flores que habían besado momentos antes. El artista único, el hombre que había fascinado a las jóvenes de las cinco partes del mundo, dormía el último sueño ante la angustia de millones de almas. Un caballero de los que formaban en aquella inmensa barrera humana, exclamó gravemente: '¡El cine está de luto! ¡El ídolo ha muerto!' (1997: 258)

[guards on foot, guards on horseback and secret police agents watched the entire path where the funeral procession was going to pass. The men respectfully took off their hats while the women, with their eyes full of tears, threw bouquets of flowers which they had kissed moments before. The artist, the man who had fascinated young women from all five parts of the world, slept his last rest before the anguish of millions of souls. One gentleman who formed part of the long human barricade gravely exclaimed: 'Film is in mourning! The idol has died!']

It is in this last chapter that the protagonist takes his own life. The fictional obituary of a beloved film star is an especially cruel comparison with the description of the death and funeral of Álvaro, himself an actor, who is buried in a common grave. The only attendees are his friend Felipe and an uncle he barely knew. The last words spoken over his body are: "Echaremos cal. Así se descompone antes" [We'll throw lye on him. That way he'll decompose faster] (1997: 381). *Cinematógrafo* is full of these Eisensteinian montages and juxtapositions.[10] On their own these fragments do not hold any apparent meaning. Read one after the other, however, they play on the contraposed emotions of the reader and produce an overall impression of disorientation and unease. Like a film editor, Carranque de Ríos expertly controls the pace of the novel by gradually shortening the

---

10. 'The essence of cinema does not lie in the images, but in the relation between the images,' according to Eisenstein (1949: 146). Eisenstein sought a deeply psychological reaction in his film viewers and would place one image next to another which separately seem to hold no meaning, but together combine to form a third concept.

fragments until the reading is propelled forward at a breakneck pace towards the end, when the death of Álvaro has a dramatic impact and represents the end of an era, an era of hope in technological progress, in the humane, well-meaning goals of Madrid's modernization found in the rhetoric of the politicians and philosophers of the time.

Eugenio de Nora refers to the narrative of *Cinematógrafo* as "un fragmentismo anárquico" [an anarchic fragmentation] (1997: 482). Yet *Cinematógrafo*'s difficult structure is an ideal tool to communicate the nature of modern time/space compression and the relationship between capital, culture and space. This underlying process is precisely what Carranque de Ríos seeks to expose in *Cinematógrafo* not just through the novel's content but through its form. The novel is comprised of many genres: the short magazine articles mentioned above, a first-person manuscript left by Álvaro (which exists in the novel because he wrote it and then presumably failed to get it published), a third-person narrator's account of how he found this first-person manuscript and how and why he decided to present it to us, the readers, as well as other sections narrated in the first person by doña Luisa and Felipe. Throughout the novel the same events are told from differing points of view and there is little sense of chronological order. These effects, combined with both formal and informal ways of speaking, the presence of both description and dialogue and the use of Madrid slang and idiomatic expressions, produce an experience like that of being on a city street and listening to the conversations of the passersby. Indeed, according to Fortea, Carranque de Ríos wrote much of *Cinematógrafo* sitting in the "El gato negro" [The Black Cat] café located on the Plaza Mayor (1997: 63-65).

During the first part of the twentieth century the word *cinematógrafo* referred to the person creating and manipulating photographic images to produce a film but also to the place—the theater—where the films were shown. With this double meaning in mind, *Cinematógrafo*, with its constant attention to specific spaces and places in Madrid, becomes a running commentary on the construction of the city's urban environment in all of its contradictions. The novel offers a critique of the official, highly visible discourses of modernity, exposing what lies beneath the façade of economic and social progress. It is also an assessment of the artist and the city in which he or she lives. Carranque de Ríos chooses to delve into the other side of this discourse of modernity: the messy, human side that goes unchronicled by the popular press, unrecognized by government and unarticulated by most avant-garde intellectuals. Carranque de Ríos and the other authors discussed in this study are important exceptions to both the avant-garde and Hollywood-based, market-driven cultural modes. Their works exemplify what Díaz Fernández in his collection of essays *El nuevo romaticismo* calls

> el nuevo romanticismo.... yo lo auguro para el arte y para la vida. Europa ya no puede más de cansancio, de escepticismo y de desconcierto. Dicen que el alma no puede vivir sin una religión. Nosotros, hijos del siglo más científico y mecanizado, hemos extirpado quizá toda clase de mitos y simbolismos; pero no podemos vivir sólo para esto, para esto tan breve, tan personal, tan egoísta y tan efímero. Necesitamos vivir para el más allá. No para el más allá del mundo, puesto que no es posible creer en una tierra detrás de las estrellas, sino para el más allá del tiempo. Es decir; necesitamos vivir para la historia, para las generaciones venideras.... Lo que se llamó vanguardia literaria en los últimos años, no era sino la postrera etapa de una sensibilidad en liquidación. La verdadera vanguardia será aquella que ajuste sus formas nuevas de expresión a las nuevas inquietudes del pensamiento. Saludemos al nuevo romanticismo del hombre y la máquina que *harán un arte para la vida, no una vida para el arte.* (1930: 48-50, italics mine)

> the new romanticism .... I foresee it for art and for life. Europe has had enough of exhaustion, of asceticism and of decay. They say that the soul cannot live without religion. We, sons of the most scientific and mechanized of centuries, have eliminated all kinds of myths and symbols; but we cannot live just for this, for the brief, the individual, the self-centered and the ephemeral. We need to live for the beyond. Not for that which is beyond the world, since it is impossible to believe in a world beyond the stars, but for that which is on the other side of time. In other words; we need to live for history, for future generations.... What was called the literary avant-garde in recent years was nothing more than the latest stage of a waning sensibility. The true avant-garde will be that which adjusts its new forms of expression to the new unsettledness of thought.

Let's welcome the new romanticism of man and machine which will *create an art for life, not a life for art.*]

Carranque de Ríos created socially conscious works which were commentaries on the urban environment in which he worked and lived. Writing socially progressive novels using avant-garde techniques and styles, he narrates both the promises and the limits of modernity during this fast-changing period of the city's modernization.

Álvaro Giménez, in an unexpected twist of the plot, ends his life by throwing himself off of the viaduct at the crossroads of the Calle de Segovia and the Calle de Bailén. One can speculate on the possible reasons for this desperate act. One is that Álvaro feels betrayed by his friend, the always-obtuse Felipe who does not understand the severity of Álvaro's economic troubles. The breaking point in their relationship seems to come when Felipe, afraid Doña Luisa is not romantically interested in him because he is overweight, asks the starving Álvaro, "–¿Tú sabes algo que haga adelgazar?" ['Do you know of anything to make you lose weight?'] to which Álvaro responds bitterly and incredulously, "—Para adelgazar existen muchas cosas" ['There are a lot of things that make you lose weight'] (1997: 361). After quitting one job writing political speeches for a lying and avaricious politician, the very last straw for Álvaro seems to come when he is fired from his job as a model at an art school. He is in severe economic need and has not eaten for days when he decides to go to the school to model as a last resort. He strips off his clothing and

> todo desnudo, esperó subido en la plataforma. A unos tres metros las caras de los alumnos le miraban a través de la niebla que producía el foco pendido sobre su cabeza…. Álvaro no pudo aguantar aquellas miradas. Al bajar los ojos vio que tenía los pies sucios. Se le indicó que girara lentamente. Álvaro creía que alguien se reía y que la risa era de mujer. Un sudor frío empezó a bajar por la frente. Se volvió a repetir la risa. Entonces el director hizo un gesto de enfado. Álvaro temía que iba a marearse. –¿No ha oído que se vaya de ahí? –le dijo el empleado. –Se le avisará en cuanto haya una posición—prometió el del guardapolvos. (1997: 377)

totally nude, he waited on top of the platform. Three meters away the
faces of the students looked at him through the fog that was created by
the light bulb hanging over his head.... Álvaro couldn't stand those
looks. When he lowered his eyes he noticed that his feet were dirty. They
told him to turn slightly. Álvaro thought that he heard someone laughing and that the laughter belonged to a woman. Then the director made
an angry gesture. Álvaro thought that he was going to faint. –Haven't
you heard that you need to go? –an employee said to him. –We'll let you
know when there is an open spot—promised the man wearing the
dustcoat.'

This scene, with the mention of the word "plataforma" [platform] to
describe the stage on which Álvaro stands recalls the dancing chickens of the beginning of the novel and simultaneously echoes back to
the scene in the Casino in Manzanares. The degradation is complete
this time, however. Unable to wash more than his face and hands for
weeks because he has no home, Álvaro is unemployable. He sees no
way out of his poverty. He has been stripped down to his very basic
essentials, made into an object for others to use and found ridiculous.
Unlike Pablo Gómez's chickens and the hopeful child actor Tony,
Álvaro is all too conscious of what lies behind his exploitation and he
finds this truth to be unbearable.

Dehumanized to the extreme, while walking home

> no se daba cuenta que había llegado al final de la Calle Mayor. Podía
> continuar por dos sitios. Por la izquierda o por la derecha. Decidió
> hacerlo por la izquierda. Por el Viaducto pasaba la gente metiendo poco
> ruido. Álvaro se aproximó a la barbadilla, puso un pie en los hierros, y
> antes de que llegaran a alcanzarlo, estaba subido en la parte alta de la
> verja..... fue demasiado tarde para impedir que Álvaro se dejara caer.
> (1997: 378-79)

[he didn't realize that he had come to the end of the Calle Mayor. He
could continue by going two different ways. To the right or to the left.
He decided to go left. People were passing through the Viaduct not making much noise. Álvaro approached the railing, put his feet on the iron
bars, and before they reached him, he was on top of the highest part of
the barrier ... it was too late to keep Álvaro from falling.]

It is significant that Álvaro decides to end his life precisely here because
when *Cinematógrafo* was written the viaduct was a recently-constructed
structure built with the latest, most technologically-advanced of engi-
neering techniques and materials.[11] Álvaro is an intelligent young man
unable to find his place in a supposedly open, fast-moving urban environment full of possibilities. Both the newly-acquired values and the
old class inequalities still present in modern Madrid are clearly indict-
ed in the novel and are seen as forces subjugating any potential for
rejuvenation, reform or progress.

At the end of the novel the unethical film entrepreneur Norberto
Robledal is reading the notice of Álvaro's suicide in a newspaper in an
office high up in a building on the Gran Vía. The article indignantly
claims that "día por día venimos diciendo que se vigile y hasta se pro-
híba, si es necesario, la mala literatura, las películas inmorales y todo
cuanto envenena a la juventud española. El suicidio desgraciado de
Álvaro Giménez es un aviso que Dios hace a los que tienen a su cargo
la gobernación de la España católica" (1997: 380) [every day we say
that bad literature, immoral films and everything that poisons the
young Spaniards of today should be guarded and even banned, if necessary. The disgraceful suicide of Álvaro Giménez is a warning to
those who take charge of governing Catholic Spain.] *Cinematógrafo* is
about the human cost of modern development, about the people left
behind in an increasingly industrialized, urban Madrid. Culture is
bound to capital, it is clear, and those involved in the production of
popular urban culture during the 1920s and 1930s were involved in
the construction of the façade of new ideologies of progress and
modernity. The media blaming Álvaro's suicide on the immorality of

---

11. One of the reasons the viaduct on the Calle de Bailén which runs over the Calle
    de Segovia was so important is that its construction in 1931 was granted to the
    best entry in a competition managed by the relatively new, prestigious, and high-
    profile Colegio de Arquitectos. According to the *Guía de Arquitectura y Urbanis-
    mo de Madrid* it was widely publicized in Madrid newspapers and much was
    made of the fact that it would be made with the newest of building techniques
    from Germany and the United States (107).

popular culture is supremely ironic, since Álvaro's desire as a journalist was to tell the truth about the city in which he lived.

In 1936 Carranque de Ríos died of cancer at the age of thirty-four
at the outbreak of the Spanish Civil War. His few literary works have
never fit easily into the categories traditionally used to organize the
study of literature in Spain. This spatial approach to his work demonstrates that his voice is both a product of and comment upon an
increasingly modern, industrial Madrid during a period of radical
urban change. The grim portrayal of the suicide of Álvaro Giménez is
symbolic of what was about to happen to the city of Madrid during
the Civil War and under the dictatorship of Francisco Franco. None
of the technology, none of the exciting possibilities for new urban
identities could save the protagonist, who represents the future and
hopes of a newly-modernizing country.

Conclusions

In his book *How to Lie with Maps* Mark Monmonier wants to "make readers aware that maps, like speeches and paintings, are authored collections of information and are also subject to distortions arising from ignorance, greed, ideological blindness, or malice" (1996: 5). We tend to take great stock in maps, which are as prone to the spatial imaginary as narrative fiction. The maps used in chapters Three, Four and Five were created for the purpose of illustrating and visualizing the relationships between the locations where the events of the novels take place and to help us draw conclusions about the importance of how the characters move through urban space. They were created using base maps of what contemporary urban historians consider to be the "best" or most legible maps available. [1] This study has attempted to map the geographical imaginaries of three novels which take different perspec-

---

1. See López de Lucio for information on the historical importance, cartographic value and use of the 1910 Núñez Granes map used as a base map in Chapter Three. Note that the 1925 map used as a base for the relational diagrams for the discussion of *La Venus mecánica* was made for the purpose of promoting commerce and a sense of rapid expansion in that it outlined neighborhoods that did not yet exist. The 1940 map, made by Falangists with German support in the wake of their victory over Republican Spain, is considered one of the best and most accurate of Madrid in the mid- to late 1930s.

tives on the experience of living in Madrid in the early part of the twentieth century. The novels provide us with critiques of the process of
modernization wreaking havoc on the lives of those caught in the middle of what was a violent and dynamic time. These modern novels sold
well and were consumed by a local reading public. Because they were
not as closely tied to capital as some other forms of artistic creation
such as architecture, urban planning and film, they had the freedom to
create alternately utopian and dystopian worlds with their social criticism in ways that films and buildings could not. In contrast to the
ambitious and revolutionary plans for the rationalization of space of
the urban planners and architects discussed in Chapter Two, these narratives were more modest but simultaneously more free to invent urban
worlds in which their readers could recognize themselves.

Moretti calls this type of literary analysis "distant reading." The spatial realities of the texts examined here have undergone a deliberate
process of abstraction and reduction. The maps (interpretative fictions
of their own) purposefully force the reader to take a step back in order
to consider what it is the work is saying about how people move and
relate to one another geographically, and how the characters are either
free to move or are bound within urban space. If we take into consideration what Lefebvre and Harvey have to say about the cartographic
imagination and the production of modern space in the city, we see
that social (Lefebvre would call it abstract) space is constantly being
created in the image of capital. This process has a real human cost and
the cartographic arguments in these novels present it for the reader's
consideration.

In Burgos's prose we read about Madrid's newly-arrived migrants
who learn how to adapt to their new environments. We see how the
city's commerce (official and unofficial) is centered around the Puerta
del Sol and the different types of activities that take place in the relatively small concentric circles around this geographical center. We also
learn about how the female body is categorized, used and discarded in
the city which has a structured system of social, medical and civil institutions that determine where a woman can and cannot be present in the
city. Working-class women are inherently public: on the city street, in
parks and therefore exposed to a variety of dangers simply because their

bodies are seen as available for consumption in the form of labor, sex and a source of visual pleasure. Burgos humanizes the faces of the masses of young women who moved to Madrid out of necessity, looking for new identities in a city desperately looking for a modern identity for itself.

Díaz Fernández emphasizes these same problems, but in a different way. By opposing very different male and female experiences of living in the same spaces in *La Venus mecánica*, the author is able to enter more deeply into the reasons behind the gender inequalities and double standards of the time. Written ten years after the Burgos texts, we see how the center of the city no longer lies in the Puerta del Sol but in the more cosmopolitan, less *castizo* Gran Vía, which sought to model itself after the great boulevards of other modern cities such as Paris, Berlin and New York. The sense of alienation is much greater in the 1920s prose, as the protagonists see themselves as anonymous figures against a theatrical backdrop, caught in the image-making film, fashion and journalism industries. The protagonists find themselves at the end of the novel in the bowels of the city, having been discarded for trying to find more real, human solutions to the social ills plaguing them and their fellow citizens.

The Madrid described by the narrators of *Cinematógrafo* in the following decade, the 1930s, chronicles a certain experience of the northern push that took place with the urban planning of Zuazo and Jensen. The Gran Vía is featured prominently as the center of leisure and commerce: a playground for the middle and moneyed classes. Meanwhile, the neighborhoods around the Rastro are overcrowded and unsanitary. When the protagonists attempt to gain access to new institutions of power and culture (the Biblioteca Nacional, the offices of the fledgling Spanish film industry, the newly-constructed luxurious residential buildings on the Calle Princesa) they encounter social or physical obstacles that greatly limit their possibilities. Social mobility is linked to spatial mobility, and both are determined by class.

Madrid between 1900 and 1936 is the center of an incredibly dynamic and diverse number of social and cultural debates. The tension between tradition and the modern, between the local and the global, would result in an unprecedented number of overlapping artistic tendencies that make characterizing the cultural production of the period a challenge. Hispanists have a weakness for labeling and defining, for dividing its authors into generations, nationalities and strict gendered categories that limit the ways we can talk about the literature of the early twentieth century. We often try to define Spain's modernity in relation to the modernities of other countries, trying to place Spain in some kind of modern hierarchy where Madrid (especially in comparison to its rival, Barcelona) will at best be peripheral. One hope for this study is that this spatial, geographical approach, or "distant reading," will loosen these stiff and rusty categories, if only for a moment.

Of all the possible texts written between 1900 and 1936 about Madrid, why study these three? First of all, each work represents a different moment in the plans for Madrid being implemented in the three decades encompassing the time period considered here. Each has different perspectives on the experience of the modern urbanization process in Madrid. Only after I had finished this study did I realize that there were certain commonalities between the authors. Burgos ("La Divorciadora," "La Dama Roja," Mason, pacifist, feminist, single mother) thrived on controversy and made a name for herself as a libertine in the predominantly male environment in which she worked as a journalist. Díaz Fernández was an important critic of the cultural conservatism of Ortega y Gasset and one of the most important radical intellectuals of his time. Carranque de Ríos, for all of his contradictions, maintained his anarchist politics until his untimely death. As I mentioned in Chapter Two, some of the world's most successful urban planners also had anarchist leanings but found that their politics were altered when they looked for investors. What is precisely so appealing and surprising about these authors is that they offer ephemeral, paper visions of urban possibilities that never existed yet incited urban dwellers to imagine new worlds for themselves. This type of reciprocal relationship between the word and the world took place in spaces that were not mere containers but ongoing social constructs. The Civil War would forever alter the experience of modernity in Spain, but the ideas about the limits and possibilities of modern urban life in circulation during this period would remain in the cultural imaginary for others to draw upon in the future.

Works Cited

BAKER, Edward (1991): *Materiales para escribir Madrid: Literatura y espacio urbano de Moratín a Galdós*. Madrid: Siglo XXI.

BAKHTIN, Mikhail Mikhailovich (1981): *The Dialogic Imagination*. Trans. Caryl Emerson and Michael Holquist. Austin: University of Texas Press.

BARNARD, Malcolm (1996): *Fashion as Communication*. London/New York: Routledge.

BELLVER, Catherine G. (1997): "Literary Influence and Female Creativity: The Case of Two Women Poets of the Generation of 27", *Siglo XX/20th Century* 15.1-2, 7-32.

BENJAMIN, Walter (1968): "The Work of Art in the Age of Mechanical Reproduction", in: Arendt, Hannah, (ed.): *Illuminations*. Trans. Harry Zohn. New York: Schocken Books, 217-252.

BERMAN, Marshall (1982): *All That Is Solid Melts Into Air. The Experience of Modernity*. New York: Penguin Books.

BERNSTEIN, Richard (ed.) (1985): *Habermas on Modernity*. Cambridge: MIT Press.

BIEDER, Maryellen (1996): "Self-Reflexive Fiction and the Discourse of Gender in Carmen de Burgos", *Bucknell Review of Literature* 39.2, 73-89.

BLANCO AGUINAGA, Carlos/Rodríguez Puertolas, Julio/Zavala, Iris M. (eds.) (1979): *Historia social de la literatura española*. Madrid: Castalia.

BOETSCH, Laurent (1985): *José Díaz Fernández y la otra generación del 27.* Madrid: Pliegos.

BOHIGAS, Oriol (1998): *Modernidad en la arquitectura de la España republicana.* Barcelona: Tusquets.

BOURDIEU, Pierre (1977): *Outline of a Theory of Practice.* Trans. Richard Nice. Cambridge/New York: Cambridge University Press.

BREWARD, Christopher (1996): *The Culture of Fashion.* Manchester: Manchester University Press.

BUÑUEL, Luis (1927): "Metropolis", review of the Fritz Lang film, in: *La Gaceta Literaria* 1.9 (May 1), 6.

BÜRGER, Peter (1984): *Theory of the Avant-Garde.* Trans. Michael Shaw. Minneapolis: University of Minnesota Press.

DE BURGOS, Carmen (1909): "Autobiografía", *Prometeo* 2, 53.

— (1927): La mujer moderna y sus derechos. Valencia: Sempere.

— (1989a): "Los negociantes de la Puerta del Sol", in Núñez Rey, Concepción (ed.): *La flor de la playa y otras novelas cortas.* Madrid: Castalia.

— (1917): *La rampa.* Madrid: Renacimiento.

— (1989b): "El veneno del arte", in: Núñez Rey, Concepción (ed.): *La flor de la playa y otras novelas cortas.* Madrid: Castalia.

CABERO, Juan Antonio (1949): *Historia de la cinematografía española 1896-1949.* Madrid: Gráficas Cinema.

CANO BALLESTA, Juan (1981): *Literatura y tecnología. Las letras españolas ante la revolución industrial (1900-1933).* Madrid: Orígenes.

CAPEL MARTÍNEZ, Rosa María (ed.) ([2]1986): *Mujer y sociedad en España 1700-1975.* Madrid: Ministerio de Cultura. Instituto de la Mujer.

— (1986): *El trabajo y la educación de la mujer en España (1900-1930).* Madrid: Ministro de la Cultura.

CARR, Raymond (1980): *Modern Spain 1875-1980.* Oxford/New York: Oxford University Press.

— /Fusi, Juan Pablo (1979): *Spain: Dictatorship to Democracy.* London: George Allen and Unwin.

CARRANQUE DE RÍOS, Andrés (1936): *Cinematógrafo.* Madrid: Espasa Calpe.

—. *Cinematógrafo* (1997): Introduction. Antonio Muñoz Molina. Madrid: Viamonte, i-xii.

— (1998): *Obra completa de Carranque de Ríos.*Fortea, José Luis (ed.). Madrid: Ediciones del Imán.

— (1934): *Uno.* Madrid: Espasa Calpe.

— (1935): *La vida difícil.* Espasa-Calpe.

— (2005): *La vida difícil.* Madrid: Cátedra.

CASTAÑAR, Fulgencio (1992): *El compromiso en la novela de la II República*. Madrid: Siglo XXI.

— (1993): "La España del siglo XX en la narrativa del compromiso", *Letras Peninsulares* 6.1, 69-82.

CASTAÑEDA, Paloma (1994): *Carmen de Burgos "Colombine"*, Madrid: Dirección General de la Mujer.

CAVALLO, Susana (1993): "El feminismo y la novela social de los años treinta", *Letras Peninsulares* 6.1, 169-178.

CHARPENTIER SAITZ, Herlinda (1990): "Carmen de Burgos-Seguí (Colombine), escritora española digna de ser recordada", in: Erro-Orthmann, Nora/Mendizabal, Juan Cruz (eds.): *La escritora hispánica. Actas de la decimotercera conferencia anual de literatura hispánica en Indiana University de Pennsylvania*. Miami: Universal, 169-179.

CHOCARRO, Carlos (2005): "José Díaz Fernández y Ortega. Literatura, arte y política (1925-1936)", *DC: Revista de Crítica Arquitectónica* 13-14, 162-173.

CHUECA, Federico/VALVERDE, Joaquín (1886): *La Gran Vía. Revista madrileña cómico-lírica, fantástico-callejera en un acto*. Madrid.

CIALLELLA, Louise (2007): *Quixotic Modernities: Reading Gender in Tristana, Trigo and Martínez Sierra*. Lewisburg: Bucknell University Press. *Cinemedia. Enciclopedia del cine español* (1997): CD-ROM. Madrid: Sogecable.

COOPER, Juan Xiros (2004): *Modernism and the Culture of Market Society*. Cambridge/New York: Cambridge University Press.

DEL CORRAL, José (2002): *La Gran Vía. Historia de una calle*. Madrid: Sílex.

CORTIZO, María Encina/SOBRINO, Eduardo (1997): Introduction. *La Gran Vía. Revista madrileña cómico-lírica, fantástico-callejera en un acto*. Madrid: SGAE. i-xxix.

CRAIK, Jennifer (1994): *The Face of Fashion: Cultural Studies in Fashion*. New York: Routledge.

CRISTÓBAL, Gloria Nielfa (1986): "Las mujeres en el comercio madrileño del primer tercio del siglo XX", en: Capel Martínez, Rosa María (ed.): *Mujer y sociedad en España 1700-1975*. Madrid: Ministerio de la Cultura, 299-322.

DAVIDSON, Robert A. (2006): "The Politicization of Jazz Age Space in José Díaz Fernández's *La Venus mecánica*", *Revista de Estudios Hispánicos* 40, 197-215.

DAVIES, Catherine (1998): *Spanish Women's Writing 1849-1996*. London: Athlone.

DEARSTYNE, Howard (1986): *Inside the Bauhaus*. New York: Rizzoli.

DÍAZ FERNÁNDEZ, José (1976): *El blocao*. Madrid: Turner.

— (1930): *El nuevo romanticismo*. Madrid: Zeus.

— (1929): *La Venus mecánica*. Madrid: Renacimiento.

DE DIEGO, Estrella (1986): "Buscando a Hollywood desesperadamente", in: *El cinematógrafo en Madrid 1896-1960*. Madrid: Ayuntamiento de Madrid and Concejalía de Cultura, 1986. Catalogue of an exhibit in the Museo Municipal March-April, 1986.

DIÉGUEZ PATAO, Sofía (1997): *La Generación del 25. Primera arquitectura moderna en Madrid*. Madrid: Cátedra.

— (1991): *Un nuevo orden urbano: "El Gran Madrid" (1939-1951)*. Madrid: Ayuntamiento de Madrid.

EISENSTEIN, Sergei (1949): *Film Form. Essays in Film Theory*. Trans. Jay Leyda. New York: Harcourt.

ESTABLIER PÉREZ, Helena (2000): *Mujer y feminismo en la narrativa de Carmen de Burgos "Colombine"*. Almería: Instituto de Estudios Almerienses.

— (1997): *La Eva moderna. Ilustración gráfica española 1914-1935*. Exhibition Catalogue. Madrid: Fundación MAPFRE Vida.

FELSKI, Rita (1995): *The Gender of Modernity*. Cambridge: Harvard University Press.

FERNÁNDEZ CIFUENTES, Luis (1982): *Teoría y mercado de la novela en España: del 98 a la República*. Madrid: Gredos.

FERNÁNDEZ POLANCO, Aurora (1990): *Urbanismo en Madrid durante la II República 1931-1939*. Madrid: Ministerio para las Administraciones Públicas.

FERNÁNDEZ SHAW, Casto (1928): Interview. *La Gaceta Literaria* 32, 3.

FERRERAS, Juan Ignacio. (1972): *La novela por entregas (1840-1900)*. Madrid: Taurus.

FISAC, Miguel (1961): *La arquitectura popular española y su valor ante la arquitectura del futuro*. Madrid: Rivadeneyra.

FOLGUERA CRESPO, Pilar (1997): "Revolución y Restauración. La emergencia de los primeros ideales emancipadores (1868-1931)", in: Garrido González, Elisa, et al. (eds.): *Historia de la mujeres de España*. Madrid: Síntesis, 451-492.

FORTEA, José Luis (1972): *La obra de Andrés Carranque de Ríos*. Madrid: Gredos.

FUENTES, Víctor (1993): "La novela social española 1927-1936: panorámica de un diverso perfil temático y formal", *Letras Peninsulares* 6.1, 9-29.

— (1980): *La marcha al pueblo en las letras españolas 1917-1936*. Madrid: Ediciones de la Torre.

FUSI, Juan Pablo/PALAFOX, Jordi (1997): *España: 1808-1996. El desafío de la modernidad.* Madrid: Espasa Calpe.

GAINES, Jane M./HERZOG, Charlotte (eds.) (1990): *Fabrications: Costume and the Female Body.* New York: Routledge.

GALLERSTEIN, Carolyn/MCNERNY, Kathleen (eds.) (1986): *Women Writers of Spain. An Annotated Bio-Bibliographical Guide.* Westport: Greenwood.

GARRIDO GONZÁLEZ, Elisa/FOLGUERA CRESPO, Pilar/ORTEGA LÓPEZ, Margarita/SEGURA Graiño, Cristina (eds.) (1997): *Historia de las mujeres en España.* Madrid: Síntesis.

GAVARRÓN, Lola (1982): *Piel de ángel. Historias de la ropa interior femenina.* Barcelona: Tusquets.

GIMÉNEZ CABALLERO, Ernesto (1935): *Arte y Estado.* Madrid: Gráfico Universal.

GÓMEZ, Carlos de San Antonio (1996): *Veinte años de arquitectura en Madrid. La edad de plata: 1918-1936.* Madrid: Consejería de Educación y Cultura.

GÓMEZ AMAT, Carlos (1984): *Historia de la música española. Siglo XIX.* Madrid: Alianza.

GOODWAY, David (1989): *For Anarchism: History, Theory and Practice.* London/New York: Routledge.

GOULD Levine, Linda/ENGLESON MARSON, Ellen/FEIMAN WALDMAN, Gloria (eds.) (1993): *Spanish Women Writers. A Bio-Bibliographical Source Book.* Westport: Greenwood.

GRAHAM, Helen/LABANYI, Jo (eds.) (1995): *Spanish Cultural Studies. An Introduction. The Struggle for Modernity.* Oxford: Oxford University Press.

GRONOW, Jukka (1997): *The Sociology of Taste.* London: Routledge.

GUBERN, Román, et al. (^{3}2000): *Historia del cine español.* Madrid: Cátedra.

HALL, Peter (1988): *Cities of Tomorrow. An Intellectual History of Urban Planning and Design in the Twentieth Century.* Oxford/New York: Blackwell.

HARVEY, David (1990): *The Condition of Postmodernity. An Enquiry into the Origins of Cultural Change.* Oxford: Blackwell.

— (1996): *Justice, Nature and the Geography of Difference.* Oxford: Blackwell.

— (1985): *The Urban Experience.* Baltimore: The Johns Hopkins University Press.

HERZBERGER, David (1993): "Representation and Transcendence: The Double Sense of Díaz Fernández's *El nuevo romanticismo*", *Letras Peninsulares* 6.1, 83-93.

HOLLANDER, Anne (1994): *Sex and Suits*. New York: A.A. Knopf.

HORKHEIMER, Max/ADORNO, Theodor W. (1989): *Dialectic of Enlightenment*. Trans. John Cumming. New York: Continuum.

HUGHES, Robert (1991): *The Shock of the New. Art and the Century of Change*. London: Thames and Hudson.

HUYSSEN, Andreas (1986): "Mass Culture as Woman: Modernism's Other", in: *After the Great Divide: Modernism, Mass Culture, Postmodernism*. Bloomington: Indiana University Press.

— (1982): "The Vamp and the Machine: Technology and Sexuality in Fritz Lang's *Metropolis*", *New German Critique* 24-25, 221-237.

JENKINS, Stephen (1981): *Fritz Lang, the Image and the Look*. London: BFI Publishers.

JENSEN, Paul M. (1969): *The Cinema of Fritz Lang*. New York: A.S. Barnes.

JOHNSON, Roberta (1993): *Crossfire: Philosophy and the Novel in Spain, 1900-1934*. Lexington, KY: University Press of Kentucky.

— (2003): *Gender and Nation in the Spanish Modernist Novel*. Nashville: Vanderbilt University Press.

JULIÁ, Santos/RINGROSE, David/SEGURA, Cristina (1995): *Madrid. Historia de una capital*. Madrid: Alianza.

LABANYI, Jo (2007): "Memory and Modernity in Democratic Spain: The Difficulty of Coming to Terms with the Spanish Civil War", *Poetics Today* 28.1, 89-116.

LANG, Fritz (1927): *Metropolis*. Berlin: UFA.

LARSON, Susan (2006): Introduction. *La rampa*. By Carmen de Burgos. Buenos Aires: StockCero, vii – xxiv.

— (2007): "Nemesio M. Sobrevila, Walter Benjamin and the Provocation of Film", *Studies in Hispanic Cinema* 4.2, 107-120.

— (2005): (ed.): "Peripheral Modernities of the Spanish Novel", *Romance Quarterly* 53.2, 1-10.

LEFEBVRE, Henri (1962): *Introduction to Modernity*. Trans. John Moore. London/New York: Verso.

— (1991): *The Production of Space*. Trans. Donald Nicholson-Smith. Oxford: Blackwell.

— (1972): *La revolución urbana*. Trans. Mario Nolla. Madrid: Alianza.

LIPOVETSKY, Gilles (1994): *The Empire of Fashion*. Trans. Catherine Porter. Princeton: Princeton University Press.

LÓPEZ DE LUCIO, Ramón (1986): "Núñez Granes y la urbanización del extrarradio en el primer tercio del Siglo XX", in: *Gestión urbanística europea 1920-1940*. Madrid: Ayuntamiento de Madrid, 73-87.

LÓPEZ-CAMPILLO, Evelyne (1972): *La "Revista de Occidente" y la formación de minorías 1923-1936*. Madrid: Taurus.

LOUIS, Anja (2005): *Women and the Law: Carmen de Burgos, an Early Feminist*. Rochester, NY: Tamesis.

MANGINI, Shirley (1995): "The Many Exiles of Rosa Chacel", in: Paolini, Claire J. (ed.): *La Chispa '95: Selected Proceedings*. New Orleans: Louisiana Conference on Hispanic Languages and Literatures, 221-229.

— (2001): *Las modernas de Madrid: Las grandes intelectuales españolas de la vanguardia*. Barcelona: Península.

MAURE RUBIO, Lilia (1986): *Anteproyecto del trazado viario y urbanización de Madrid: Zuazo-Jansen, 1929-1930*. Madrid: Colegio Oficial de Arquitectos.

MONMONIER, Mark (^{2}1996): *How to Lie with Maps*. Chicago: University of Chicago Press.

MORETTI, Franco (2005): *Graphs, Maps, Trees. Abstract Models for a Literary History*. London and New York: Verso.

MORRIS, C.B. (1980): *This Loving Darkness. The Cinema and Spanish Writers 1920-1936*. Oxford: Oxford University Press.

NADAL, Jordi (1987): "A Century of Industrialization in Spain, 1833-1930", in: Sánchez Albornoz, Nicolás (ed.): *The Economic Modernization of Spain*. Trans. Powers, Karen/Sañudo, Manuel. New York: New York University Press.

— (1984): *La población española: Siglos XVI a XX*. Barcelona: Ariel.

NASH, Mary (1983): *Mujer, familia y trabajo en España (1875-1936)*. Barcelona: Anthropos.

— (1999): "Un/contested Identities: Motherhood, Sex Reform and the Modernization of Gender Identity in Early Twentieth-Century Spain", in: Enders, Victoria Lorée Enders/Radcliff, Pamela Beth (eds.): *Constructing Spanish Womanhood: Female Identity in Modern Spain*. Stonybrook: State University of New York Press, 25-50.

NAYLOR, Gillian (1986): *The Bauhaus*. London: Studio Vista.

NELKEN, Margarita (1922): *La condición social de la mujer en España*. Barcelona: Minerva.

NORA, Eugenio G. de (^{2}1979): *La novela española contemporánea (1927-1939)*. Madrid: Gredos.

NÚÑEZ REY, Concepción (2005): *Carmen de Burgos, Colombine, en la Edad de Plata de la literatura española*. Sevilla: Fundación José Manuel Lara.

— (1989): Introduction. *La flor de la playa y otras novelas cortas*. Madrid: Editorial Castalia. i-xxiii.

PARSONS, Deborah L. (2003): *A Cultural History of Madrid. Modernism and the Urban Spectacle*. Oxford: Berg.

PÉREZ, Janet (1988): *Contemporary Women Writers of Spain*. Boston: Twayne Publishers.

— (1993): "On Misapplications of the Generational Label", *Letras Peninsulares* 6.1, 31-50.

PÉREZ ROJAS, Francisco Javier (1986): "Los cines madrileños: del barracón al rascacielos", in: *El cinematógrafo en Madrid 1896-1960*. 69-83. Madrid: Ayuntamiento de Madrid and Concejalía de Cultura, 69-83.

— (1997): "Introduction", in: *La Eva moderna. Ilustración gráfica española entre 1914 y 1935*. Madrid: Fundación Cultural MAPFRE Vida.

PERUCHA, Julio Pérez (1997): *Antología crítica del cine español 1906-1995*. Madrid: Cátedra/Filmoteca Española.

PINKNEY, David H. (1985): *Napoleon III and the Rebuilding of Paris*. Princeton: Princeton University Press.

PINTO CRESPO, Virgilio (ed.) (2002): *Madrid. Átlas histórico de la ciudad, 1850-1939*. Madrid: Caja Madrid and Lunwerg.

POGGIOLI, Renato (1968): *The Theory of the Avant-Garde*. Trans. Gerald Fitzgerald. Cambridge: Harvard University Press.

REED, Donald R.C. (1997): *Following Kohlberg: Liberalism and the Practice of Democratic Community*. South Bend, IN: University of Notre Dame Press.

RESINA, Joan Ramon (2008): *Barcelona's Vocation of Modernity. Rise and Decline of an Urban Image*. Stanford: Stanford University Press.

RICCI, Cristián (2009): *El espacio urbano del Madrid en la narrativa de la Edad de Plata (1900-1938)*. Madrid: CSIC.

RODRÍGUEZ, María Pilar (1997): "Desviación y perversion en 'El veneno del arte' de Carmen de Burgos", *Symposium* 51.3, 172-185.

— (1988): "Modernidad y feminismo: tres relatos de Carmen de Burgos", *Anales de la Literatura Española Contemporánea* 23, 379-403.

SAMBRICIO, Carlos (1999): *Madrid: Ciudad-Región. De la Ciudad Ilustrada a la primera mitad del siglo XX*. Madrid: Comunidad de Madrid.

— (2003): *Madrid y sus anhelos urbanísticos. Memorias inéditas de Secundino Zuazo, 1919-1940*. Madrid: Nerea.

— / MAURE, Lilia (1984): *Madrid, urbanismo y gestión municipal 1920-1940*. Madrid: Ayuntamiento de Madrid.

SAN ANTONIO GÓMEZ, Carlos (1996): *Veinte años de arquitectura en Madrid. La edad de plata (1918-1936)*. Madrid: Comunidad de Madrid.

SANTIÁÑEZ, Nil (2007): "Mirada cartográfica y voluntad-de-arquitectura en la obra fascista de Ernesto Giménez Caballero", *Bulletin of Spanish Studies* 84.3, 325-347.

SANTONJA, Gonzalo (1993): "La primera 'novela roja'", *Letras Peninsulares* 6.1, 51-68.

— /ESTEBAN, José (1987): *La novela social 28/39. Figuras y tendencias.* Madrid: La Idea.

SCANLON, Geraldine M. (1986): *La polémica feminista en la España contemporánea 1868-1974.* Madrid: Akal.

SIMMEL, Georg (1903): "Die Großstadt und das Geistesleben" [The Metropolis and Mental Life], in: (1950): *The Sociology of Georg Simmel.* Trans. Kurt H. Wolff. Glencoe, IL: Free Press.

— (1923): "Filosofía de la moda", *Revista de Occidente* 1, 42-66.

SMITH, Neil (1984): *Uneven Development: Nature, Capital, and the Production of Space.* Athens: University of Georgia Press.

STARCEVIC, Elizabeth D. (1976): *Carmen de Burgos, defensora de la mujer.* Almería: Editorial Cajal.

SUBIRATS, Eduardo (1993): *Después de la lluvia. Sobre la ambigua modernidad española.* Madrid: Temas de Hoy.

TALENS, Jenaro/ZUNZUNEGUI, Santos (1998): "History as Narration: Rethinking Film History from Spanish Cinema", in: Talens, Jenaro/ Zunzunegui, Santos (eds.): *Modes of Representation in Spanish Cinema.* Minneapolis: University of Minnesota Press, 1-46.

TORRES, Augusto M. (1986): "De Madrid al cine. Historia del cine madrileño", in: *El cinematógrafo en Madrid 1896-1960*, Madrid: The Ayuntamiento de Madrid/Concejalía de Cultura, 19-23. Catalogue of an exhibit in the Museo Municipal de Madrid March-April, 1986.

TUÑÓN DE LARA, Manuel (1970): *Medio siglo de cultura española (1885-1936).* Madrid: Editorial Tecnos.

UGARTE, Michael (1998): "Carmen de Burgos ("Colombine"): Feminist *avant la lettre*", in: Glenn, Kathleen/Mazquiarán de Rodríguez, Mercedes (eds.): *Spanish Women Writers and the Essay. Gender, Politics and the Self.* Columbia/London: University of Missouri Press, 55-76.

— (1994): "The Generational Fallacy and Spanish Women Writing in Madrid at the Turn of the Century", *Siglo XX/20th Century* 12.1-2, 261-276.

— (1996): *Madrid 1900: The Capital as Cradle of Literature and Culture.* University Park, PA: The Pennsylvania State University Press.

URIOSTE AZCORRA, Carmen de. (1997): *Narrativa andaluza (1900-1936). Erotismo, feminismo y regionalismo*. Sevilla: Universidad de Sevilla Secretariado de Publicaciones.

URRUTIA NÚÑEZ, Ángel (1997): *Arquitectura española. Siglo XX*. Madrid: Ediciones Cátedra.

— (1992): *Arquitectura moderna: el GATEPAC*. Madrid: Información y Revistas.

WILLIAMS, Bernard (1997): *The Analogy of City and Soul in Plato's* Republic*: Critical Essays*. Lanham, MD and Oxford: Rowman and Littlefield Press.

WILSON, Elizabeth (1990): "All the Rage", in: Gaines, Jane M./Herzog, Charlotte (eds.): *Fabrications.Costume and the Female Body*. New York: Routledge, 28-38.

YORK, Peter (1984): *Modern Times: Everybody Wants Everything*. London: Heinemann Publishers.

Index

List of Illustrations

FIGURE 4.2

Blanco y negro cover by Roberto Martínez Baldrich entitled "Coquetería, 1925."

FIGURE 4.3

Cover of first edition of *La Venus mecánica* (1929), by graphic artist Ramón Puyol.

FIGURE 4.4

Map created by Dick Galbreath and Jeff Levy, University of Kentucky Gyula Pauer Center for Cartography. Historical base map source: "Nuevo Plano y Callejero de Cobrananzas: Madrid," 1925.

FIGURE 4.5

Chart of gendered spaces in *La Venus mecánica*. Created by author.

FIGURE 5.1

Carranque de Ríos head shot, 1932. Photographer unknown. Courtesy of the National Film Archives, Madrid.

FIGURE 5.2

Map created by Dick Galbreath and Jeff Levy, University of Kentucky Gyula Pauer Center for Cartography. Historical base map source: "Plano de Madrid," 1940.

FIGURE 5.3

Map created by Dick Galbreath and Jeff Levy, University of Kentucky Gyula Pauer Center for Cartography. Historical base map source: "Plano de Madrid," 1940.

Figure 1.1
Poster for Fritz Lang's *Metropolis* from *El Sol,* 22 January 1928, 5.

Figure 2.1
Photograph of construction on the Gran Vía, 1921. Photographer unknown.
Courtesy of Carlos Sambricio.

Figure 2.2
Photograph of *chabolistas* in front of the newly-constructed Plaza de Toros in Madrid, 1934. Photographer unknown. Courtesy of Carlos Sambricio.

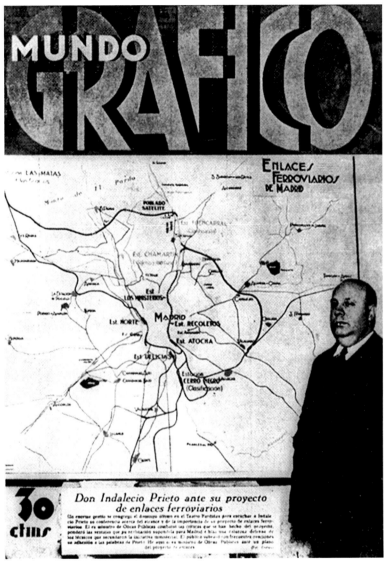

Figure 2.3
Indalecio Prieto on the cover of *Mundo Gráfico* on April 4, 1933.

Figure 2.4
Photograph of the Carrión/Capitol Building, 1933. Photographer unknown.
Courtesy of the Archive of the Municipal Museum of Madrid.

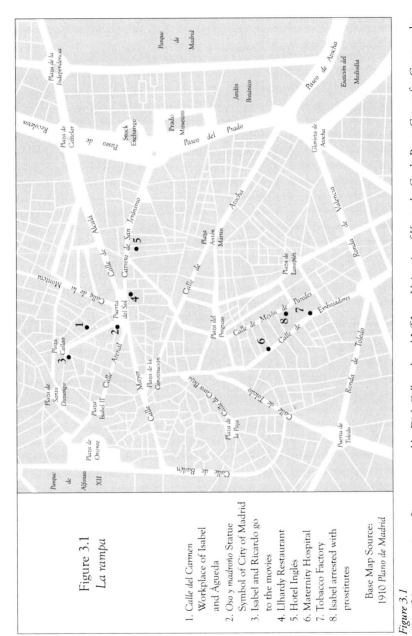

Figure 3.1
Map of *La rampa* points of interest created by Dick Galbreath and Jeff Levy, University of Kentucky Gyula Pauer Center for Cartography. Historical base map source: "Plano de Madrid," 1910.

Figure 3.1
La rampa

1. Calle del Carmen
   Workplace of Isabel
   and Águeda
2. Oso y madroño Statue
   Symbol of City of Madrid
3. Isabel and Ricardo go
   to the movies
4. Lhardy Restaurant
5. Hotel Inglés
6. Maternity Hospital
7. Tobacco Factory
8. Isabel arrested with
   prostitutes

Base Map Source:
1910 *Plano de Madrid*

Figure 4.1
Blanco y negro cover by Ramón Roqueta entitled "Portada, 1919."

Figure 4.2
Blanco y negro cover by Roberto Martínez Baldrich entitled "Coquetería, 1925."

Figure 4.3
Cover of first edition of *La Venus mecánica* (1929), by graphic artist Ramón Puyol.

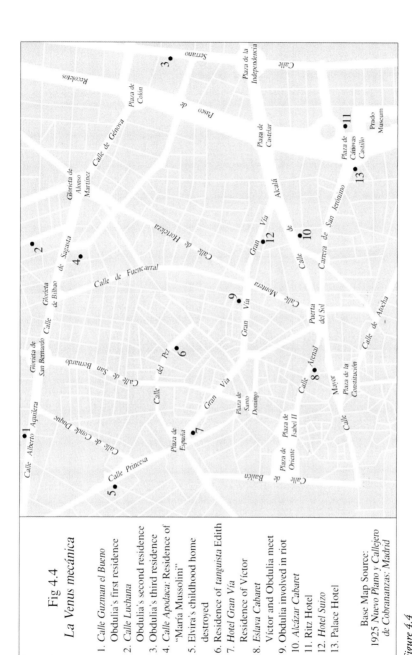

Fig 4.4
La Venus mecánica

1. *Calle Guzman el Bueno*
   Obdulia's first residence
2. *Calle Luchana*
   Obdulia's second residence
3. *Calle Apodaca*: Residence of "María Mussolini"
4. *Calle Apodaca*: Residence of "María Mussolini"
5. Elvira's childhood home destroyed
6. Residence of *tanguista* Edith
7. *Hotel Gran Vía*
   Residence of Víctor
8. *Eslava Cabaret*
   Víctor and Obdulia meet
9. Obdulia involved in riot
10. *Alcázar Cabaret*
11. *Ritz Hotel*
12. *Hotel Suizo*
13. *Palace Hotel*

Base Map Source:
1925 *Nuevo Plano y Callejero de Cobrananzas: Madrid*

Figure 4.4
Map created by Dick Galbreath and Jeff Levy, University of Kentucky Gyula Pauer Center for Cartography. Historical base map source: "Nuevo Plano y Callejero de Cobrananzas: Madrid," 1925.

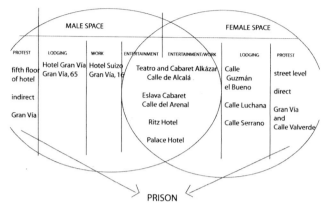

Figure 4.5
Chart of gendered spaces in *La Venus mecánica.* Created by author.

Figure 5.1
Carranque de Ríos head shot, 1932. Photographer unknown.
Courtesy of the National Film Archives, Madrid.

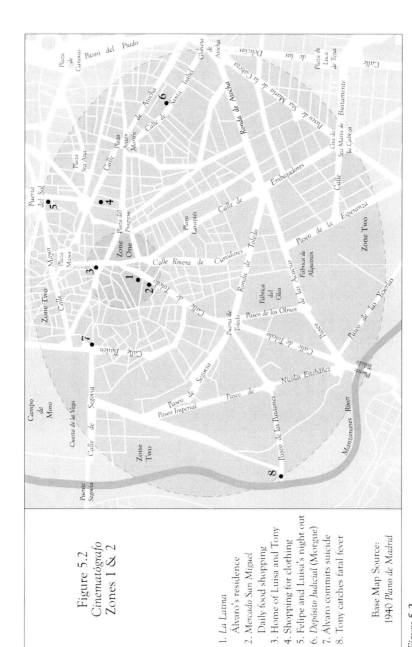

Figure 5.2
Cinematógrafo
Zones 1 & 2

1. La Latina
   Álvaro's residence
2. Mercado San Miguel
   Daily food shopping
3. Home of Luisa and Tony
4. Shopping for clothing
5. Felipe and Luisa's night out
6. Depósito Judicial (Morgue)
7. Álvaro commits suicide
8. Tony catches fatal fever

Base Map Source:
1940 *Plano de Madrid*

Figure 5.2
Map created by Dick Galbreath and Jeff Levy, University of Kentucky Gyula Pauer Center for Cartography. Historical base map source: "Plano de Madrid," 1940.

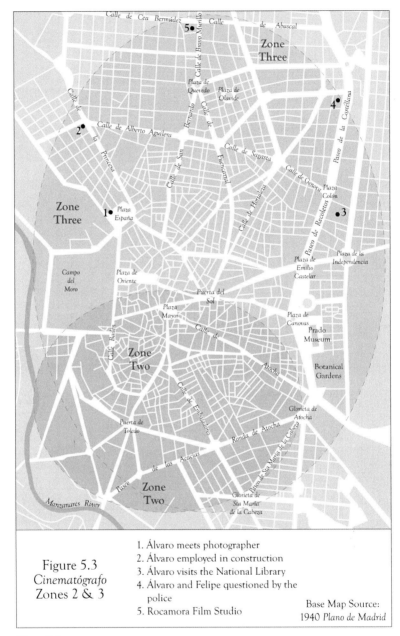

Figure 5.3
Cinematógrafo
Zones 2 & 3

1. Álvaro meets photographer
2. Álvaro employed in construction
3. Álvaro visits the National Library
4. Álvaro and Felipe questioned by the police
5. Rocamora Film Studio

Base Map Source:
1940 *Plano de Madrid*

Figure 5.3
Map created by Dick Galbreath and Jeff Levy, University of Kentucky Gyula Pauer Center for Cartography. Historical base map source: "Plano de Madrid," 1940.